The Great
Boston
Trivia & FACT
BOOK

The Great Boston Trivia & FACT BOOK

Merrill Kaitz

CUMBERLAND HOUSE

NASHVILLE, TENNESSEE

I am grateful to the following people for helping to make this book actual: Sheree Bykofsky, Ed Curtis, Jamie Jamieson, Bettie Kaitz, Haskell Kaitz, Jonah Kaitz, LaShawna Lake, Ron Pitkin, and Ann Sanfedele.

Published by Cumberland House Publishing, Inc., 431 Harding Industrial Park Drive, Nashville, Tennessee 37211-3160.

All photographs copyright Ann Sanfedele, with the following exceptions. Photographs on pages 226, 230, and 231 courtesy of the Boston Celtics. Images on pages 210 and 211 courtesy of the Boston Red Sox. Photographs on pages 166, 171, 174, 180, and 181 by the author.

Cover design by Joel Wright
Cover photographs by

Library of Congress Cataloging-in-Publication Data

    Kaitz, Merrill, 1946–
        The great Boston trivia & fact book / Merrill Kaitz.
        p. cm.
        Includes bibliographical references and index.
        ISBN 1-58182-012-7 (pbk. : alk. paper)
        1. Boston (Mass.) Miscellanea. I. Title. II. Title: Great Boston trivia and fact book.
    F73.3.K35 1999
    974.4'61—dc21
                                99-25686
                                CIP

Printed in the United States of America.

1 2 3 4 5 6 7 8 9—04 03 02 01 00 99

CONTENTS

Introduction   *vii*

1 A Dust of Snow   *3*
   Geology, geography, natural history, climate, and
   disasters natural and unnatural

2 Not Our Cup of Tea   *23*
   Boston's history to 1776

3 A Melting Pot of Beans   *39*
   Boston's history since 1776

4 Shopkeepers, Traders, and Techies   *57*
   Commerce from Cogan to Ponzi, from nails to
   Patriot missiles

5 Beacon Hill Beauties and Beasts   *87*
   The good, the bad, and the ugly in Boston politics

6 Saint Elsewhere   *105*
   Boston's institutions of science, culture, and
   the humanities

7 Transcendental Meditations   *131*
   Literature and art from Bradstreet to Emerson to
   Winslow Homer to Updike to Robert B. Parker

8 Banned in Boston   *151*
   Theater, movies, and television, from The Orphan
   to Good Will Hunting

9 Publick Occurrences   *167*
   Boston's media: newspapers, radio, and television

10 Crime and Punishment   *185*
   The underside of a Puritan city

11 Wait Till Next Year   *201*
   America's greatest sports town

Bibliography   *231*

Index   *235*

INTRODUCTION

Whether it's because they are too reserved or because it simply goes without saying, Boston natives do not plaster their bumpers with stickers that say "I love Boston." Bostonian pride, however, may run deeper than that of any other American city. Boston's landmarks and stories are very special. Most people who live in the city, or even pay close attention when they visit, seem to agree.

It wasn't always so, but as the twentieth century ends, Boston is smaller than America's giant metropolises. But Boston is also older, and it's arguably wiser. More than 10 million tourists visit Boston every year. More than 130,000 students come from elsewhere to study in Boston. Many of the students decide to stay after they graduate from one of Greater Boston's 65 universities. As a symbol of America's history and as an intellectual center, Boston is unrivaled.

Bostonians have called their city "the Athens of America," "the cradle of liberty," and, even more hyperbolically, "the hub of the universe." The newspapers frequently refer to Boston as "the Hub," for short. Residents don't say that, but they don't bat an eye when they see it in the paper.

Boston is called "the cradle of liberty" for obvious reasons. Most important is that the American Revolution started in Boston. The Sons of Liberty first discussed independence here. The slogan "Taxation without representation is tyranny" originated in Boston, and the colonists' most dramatic protest against British taxes was the Boston Tea Party, in which colonists disguised as Indians threw tea into Boston Harbor rather than pay an increased tax. The "shot heard 'round the world" that started the American Revolution was fired in Lexington, a Boston suburb. It was not a Bostonian, of course, who wrote the Declaration of Independence—but it was a Bostonian who most famously put his John Hancock on the document.

Boston was America's first major city. For a long time it was the nation's biggest city and its de facto capital. Only in the past century did archrival New York take over those distinctions, with numerous other metropolises such as Chicago, Los Angeles, and San Francisco also challenging Boston in one category or another.

But Boston's history has always been significant to the United States and even to the world. Boston's Puritan religion as well as the reactions against it continue to play a role in our national debates. The city was a major center of the movement to abolish slavery. The Irish immigration to Boston changed Boston's politics and led to the Kennedy presidency—as well as the achievements and escapades of numerous other Kennedy scions.

It's perhaps not widely recognized that Boston was the nation's business center until at least the mid-nineteenth century, when New York gradually grew dominant. No doubt Boston's continuing importance in twentieth-century business is even less acknowledged. The city remains a major player in investment, even if few people realize that the mutual fund was invented in the Hub. The presence of the Massachuseets Institute of Technology (MIT) and Harvard University helps to maintain Boston's quiet but intimate connection to the nation's—and the world's—financial development. The Internet began on the banks of the Charles.

The original "City on a Hill" is renowned for political corruption and skullduggery. Boston has certainly spawned some fascinating and shameless villains. Perhaps the most famous non-Kennedy in the group is former mayor, governor, and jailbird James Michael Curley. Curley inspired the popular novel, later a film, *The Last Hurrah*. In Boston, the debate still rages over whether Curley should be seen more as a greedy scoundrel or as a flamboyant benefactor of the common man.

If Boston's feelings are mixed regarding its presidents and scoundrels, the city's pride in its institutions of art, science, and literature is nearly pure. Bostonians justifiably consider their universities, hospitals, and literary lions to be second to none. Harvard, MIT, Brandeis, Tufts, Boston College, Boston University, and numerous other colleges and universities and the artists, scientists, and scholars who pass through these institutions make Boston one of the world's preeminent intellectual centers. The likes of Hawthorne and Emerson are near the top of the long list of Boston's major and minor writers, a list that can only be rivaled in this country by the wider territory of the American South, or by the community of writers who gather around

New York for that city's cosmopolitanism and publishing activity. But Boston's literary community continues to flourish. In spite of his life-long relationship with the *New Yorker* magazine, novelist John Updike has chosen to live most of his adult life in the Boston vicinity.

Although Boston can appear culturally provincial, even the city's parochialism has become legendary. "Banned in Boston" is a world-famous phrase that paradoxically can bestow honor on the plays, novels, and poems that earn this exalted description.

From its earliest days, Boston has had its share both of heinous criminals and of heinous inquisitors in the name of law and order. The craftsman who made the first set of stocks for publicly embarrassing wrongdoers was promptly clapped into his stocks for allegedly charging too much. Pirates, heretics, and women condemned as witches have been hanged from the majestic trees of Boston Common.

For a long time, Boston's Brinks robbers have held the record for largest cash theft. The Brinks robbery of 1950 netted $1.2 million in cash and another $1.5 million in securities, checks, and money orders. Bostonians are perversely proud that our comparatively small city, the Athens of America, spawned smalltime crooks of such prowess.

Another grand milestone of larceny occurred in Boston in 1990 when thieves stole more than $200 million worth of paintings, including a Vermeer, three Rembrandts, and five Degas, from the city's Isabella Stewart Gardner Museum. It's possible that some outlaw pride is attached to this crime as well, since it shines a spotlight on Boston's cultural resources and the sophistication of the city's rats. But the majority of civilized people, both in Boston and around the world, probably wish devoutly for the success of the ongoing investigation and the return of the loot. The Vermeer, after all, is one of only thirty-two in existence. We want to see it again. We want it back. It was stolen from all of us.

Pride is certainly not the word for our fascination with the Boston Strangler, who raped and murdered thirteen women from 1962 to 1964. Albert Desalvo was believed to be the killer, but he was not convicted for any of the Boston Strangler murders. Instead, he was imprisoned for other rapes, and many felt a sense of closure if not justice when he was stabbed to death in his cell in 1973.

Boston's sports scene offers an escape from the modern world's grimness, and it exemplifies a great deal about the city as well.

Boston's baseball team, the Red Sox, was a charter member of the American League and winner of the first World Series. Fenway Park, opened in 1912, is a historic monument of the sport and is considered, along with Wrigley Field in Chicago, a beloved and holy place to baseball aficionados.

Yet the Red Sox have not won a World Series since 1918, and the park is not expected to last much longer as a result of its aging and outmoded facilities. A bad deal in 1919, sending Babe Ruth from Boston to New York for the money to finance a musical, gave New York the ascendancy over Boston ever after. For the rest of the century Boston would come close and even win some moral victories with greats like Ted Williams and Carl Yastrzemski, but the Red Sox would not win a World Series.

Boston did achieve later glories in basketball. The Boston Celtics won seventeen championships in the latter half of the twentieth century. Pre–Michael Jordan basketball legends Red Auerbach, Bob Cousy, Bill Russell, John Havlicek, and Larry Bird helped to create one of the greatest of professional sports dynasties. But as the century nears its end, coach and team president Rick Pitino, a New Yorker with some Boston roots, struggles to rebuild the once great team. "Celtic Pride" is the team's motto, as well as the name of a recent but mediocre movie.

Boston's facts are pretty fascinating, and its trivia, at least to most Bostonians and tourists, is not all that trivial. Though the city is aging and sometimes appears to be floundering in its great rivalry with New York, its sights, events, resources, personalities, and stories keep citizens and visitors believing that Boston is still the center of the known universe.

The Great
Boston
Trivia & FACT BOOK

The Boston Common skating rink attracts a crowd at the foot of Beacon Hill.

1

A Dust of Snow

Geology, geography, natural history, climate, and disasters natural and unnatural

A cup of New England air is better than a whole draught of Old England air.

FRANCIS HIGGINSON

THE LAND, WATER, AIR, and climate of Boston can be harsh and unwelcoming, but they have inspired great devotion in residents of the area since before Europeans arrived. Tourists travel to New England from as far away as Florida and Japan to watch the autumn foliage turn. Even Hawaiians and San Franciscans have been known to envy Bostonians the turning of the four seasons.

Our blizzards and nor'easters are clearly superior to the piddling off-white soot storms experienced by the New Yorkers who live far to our south. It's true that their summer heat rivals ours—but that's only because they have so much extra asphalt and concrete to reflect and magnify it.

New England's encounters with glaciers during relatively recent geological times are fairly well known. The area's rolling hills, hollows, and granite deposits are souvenirs of the ice. Less well known, even to most of the people who live on the spot, is the existence, some 100 million years ago, of an active volcano in what is now Boston's West Roxbury neighborhood.

Even Boston's disasters, large and small, have distinctive character. Because Boston Harbor was the center of the country's shipping in its earliest days, and because merchants and mariners were bold if not reckless, our shipwrecks are legion. The loss of life is fearsome to contemplate, but the struggles and the heroism are amazing.

The city's two great fires are well known and horrifying. Our hurricanes, fortunately, are less frequent and generally less severe than those of Florida or the Caribbean, but when they arrive, their effect on the New England landscape can be beautiful and terrible.

One of the most remarkable incidents in the history and lore of Boston is the Great Molasses Flood of 1919. The event seems to astonish and to stick in the memory of everyone who hears of it, yet the details are not well known even in Boston. In mid-January, in Boston's North End, a ninety-foot tank of molasses exploded. Some two million gallons of molasses weighing more than fourteen thousand tons swept through the streets, killing 21 and injuring 150.

Referring to the Charles River, a popular rock song of the 1970s, still often heard, chanted:

> Love that dirty water
> O, O, Boston, you're my home.

The sentimental lyric summed up the feelings of numerous Bostonians.

620,000,000 B.C.

Q: What is the earliest evidence of life in Boston?
A: Fossil crustaceans of the Cambrian period, including trilobites an inch or two long, have been found in the Boston area. These provide the earliest scientific evidence of life in Boston.

500,000,000 B.C.

Boston's oldest rocks are "braintree" slates formed half a billion years ago. Much later, heat formed granites and diorite. The granite, eventually to be known in the Boston area as Quincy granite, crowded out the slate.

300,000,000 B.C.

During the Carboniferous period, glaciers reached Boston, leaving a vast lake coated with glacial clay when they melted, which under pressure became Cambridge slate.

225,000,000 B.C.

At the end of the Permian and the beginning of the Triassic periods, the continents were separating. By the end of the Triassic period, North America and Europe are thought to have separated, leaving Boston at the edge of the great ocean separating North America from Europe. Molten flows created underground "dikes" in the Boston area, and at the end of the Triassic or during the beginning of the Jurassic, these were fractured along fault lines in many places. The great Medford dike runs from Somerville three miles north to Spot Pond.

100,000,000 B.C.

Q: Where was Boston's volcano?

A: At about this time a volcano in the center of what is today West Roxbury cooled down and became inactive. The volcano was located near what is now the corner of Washington and Grove Streets.

13,000,000 B.C.

During the Pliocene epoch the land was higher, and the seashore probably extended one hundred or so miles farther east. Storms and earthquakes shaped the land into much the form it has today, except for glacial changes that occurred from 1 million to some ten thousand years ago.

1,000,000 B.C.

Q: What happened to Boston during the Ice Age?

A: The Wisconsin ice sheet swept over Boston during the Pleistocene epoch, extending at its southernmost point some one hundred miles south of Boston. The ice sheet ranged from several hundred feet to two miles high.

The ice melted slowly, leaving valleys and glacial lakes as well as Boston Bay still frozen. Gradually the drainage patterns of the Charles and Neponset Rivers were established.

15,000 B.C.

Retreating glaciers at the end of the last ice age left sand, boulders, and Boston blue clay. The glaciers also left ponds, lakes, and hills, more or less shaping the modern Boston landscape, including Beacon Hill, Bunker Hill, and the harbor islands. Under the clay is hardpan or till left by glaciers, varying from a few feet to more than one hundred feet thick. Under the hardpan is bedrock. The bedrock under most of Boston is Cambridge slate. Roxbury pudding stone lies under most of Roxbury, West Roxbury, Dorchester, Brighton, Brookline, and Newton.

Cambridge slate has been used in the construction of churches, large buildings, and house foundations, but it is rarely used today. Pudding stone was also often used as a building material, particularly in walls, arches, and bridge abutments, until it was replaced by concrete for most of these jobs.

Q: Where did Roxbury pudding stone come from?
A: One local legend says that Roxbury pudding stone was once actual pudding eaten by giants, until a mammoth food fight scattered it over the landscape.

9,000 B.C.

The Charles, a relatively young river, took on most of its present configuration. Forests dominated by black spruce established themselves in the Shawmut Peninsula.

4,000 B.C.

Oak became abundant in the Shawmut Peninsula, crowding out the pine forests.

A.D. 600

By this date most of the Indian tribes that Europeans were to encounter one thousand years later had established themselves in

New England. The most abundant tribe around Boston Harbor was the Massachusetts. South of Boston were the domains of the Wampanoags, Pokanokets, and Narragansetts. North of the harbor area lived the Agawams, Pawtuckets, and Pennacooks.

1600

Scholarly estimates suggest that some sixty thousand Native Americans lived in Massachusetts, Connecticut, Rhode Island, and New Hampshire.

1614

English explorer Capt. John Smith named Boston's river Massachusetts, after the local Indian tribe, but Prince Charles of England, who later became Charles I, changed the name to the River Charles. At this time the river's basin was a nine-mile-long tidal estuary, an area of salt marshes and mudflats that filled and emptied with the ocean's tides.

1615–20

At about this time an epidemic of bubonic plague introduced by European explorers decimated the American Indian population of New England.

1629

In times gone by the peninsula of Shawmut . . . hung from the main by a tenuous thread of marshy ground, low-lying, and barely a quarter of a mile across. To the east of this strip lay the ragged indentation of South Cove and the shallows known as Dorchester Flats. On the west was the broad expanse of Back Bay and the Roxbury Flats, forming a deep pouch in the southern shore of the Charles. . . . Beyond the narrow, swampy isthmus by which it was joined to the hills of Roxbury, Shawmut broadened and swelled, like an enormous, irregular raindrop. It rose, gradually at first, and then more abruptly, to the summits of three sharply defined hills: Copp's on the northeast, Beacon in the center, and Fort on the east.
JOHN JENNINGS, BOSTON, CRADLE OF LIBERTY, 1630–1776

Bostonians love the dirty water of the Charles River.

Q: Where did the name Boston come from?

A: Boston was at first known as Trimountain after the three central hills that rose there in colonial times. Only part of Beacon Hill remains today, the rest of the trimountain having been leveled. The Puritans named the city Boston as soon as they arrived in 1630, after the town in Lincolnshire, England, that many of them came from. The English Boston got its name from a shortening of Botolph's Town or Bot's Town. St. Botolph, appropriately for both cities, is the patron of fishermen, and the name Botolph literally means "boat-helper."

The Shawmut Peninsula got its name from the Massachusetts Indian word *Mushauwomuk*, which the English shortened to Shawmut. It means "where there is a big river."

The three hills, as well as their subsidiary peaks and ridges, had numerous names in earlier times. The eastern peak was called Pemberton, or Cotton Hill. The western, Mount Vernon, was also popularly known as Mount Whoredom. Beacon Hill was originally known as Sentry Hill but was renamed when a beacon was placed on the hill in 1634.

1630

When the Puritans arrived, there were nearly forty islands in Boston Harbor. At least eleven have disappeared. Extinct Boston Harbor islands include:

Apple Island	Half Moon Island
Bird Island	Hog Island
Castle Island	Nix's Mate
Cat Island	Noddle's Island
Deer Island	Nut Island
Governor's Island	

Remaining Boston Harbor islands include:

The Brewsters	Long Island
Bumpkin Island	Lovell's Island
Button Island	Moon Island
Calf Island	Peddock's Island
Gallop's Island	Raccoon Island
George's Island	Ragged Island
Grape Island	Rainsford Island
The Graves	Sailor Island
Green Island	Sheep Island
Hangman's Island	Slate Island
Langlee's Island	Snake Island
Lighthouse Island	Spectacle Island
Little Calf Island	Thompson's Island
Little Hog Island	

The Boston Harbor islands have a picturesque history. Their facts and lore fill many books. A few have particularly intriguing stories.

Q: What is the legend of Nix's Mate?
A: Nix's Mate and other Boston Harbor islands were used as places to hang pirates and display their bodies as warnings to

passing sailors. Legend says that Captain Nix was murdered at sea and that his first mate was hanged for the crime on Nix's Island. Before he was hanged he is said to have proclaimed his innocence, prophesying that as proof the angry sea would wash away the island. Nix's Mate was indeed washed away.

The former Castle Island is now joined by a roadway to South Boston. Throughout the eighteenth century it was the site of successive forts, ending with Fort Independence. Many disasters took place there. Guns exploded, killing their crews, and a floating wharf capsized in 1896, drowning four boys. A fatal duel was fought there on Christmas Day, 1817, and soldiers took revenge on the winner by sealing the officer alive in the spaces of a dungeon wall. Ten years later Edgar Allan Poe was stationed at the fort, and this event inspired later short stories. The body of the soldier sealed in the wall was excavated by workmen in 1905.

Deer Island was first used as a penal colony during King Philip's War, when five hundred Indians were confined there. In the first three decades of the eighteenth century, resident William Tewksbury was credited with saving thirty-one people from drowning.

Gallop's Island has had many uses; it has been farmed, used for fishing and chowder parties, served as a quarantine station, as an internment camp for German soldiers during World War II, and as a radio school for the U.S. Maritime Service.

George's Island was the site of Fort Warren, constructed between 1833 and 1850 for harbor defense. More than one thousand Confederate prisoners were held there during the Civil War.

Q: Where were the first apple trees in America planted?
A: Governor's Island, now no longer an island but part of Logan Airport, is said to have been the site of the first apple trees in America.

During the Prohibition years of the 1920s, Green Island is said to have been used by rum-runners.

Q: What was the name of America's first lighthouse?
A: Boston Light, the first lighthouse in America, was built on Lighthouse Island in 1716.

Q: What illegal athletic event was held on a Boston Harbor island?
A: Until an 1873 police raid put a stop to the practice, the harbor's biggest island, Long Island, was the site of prizefights that were banned in Boston .

Lovell's Island was not only used to pasture horses during the nineteenth century—it also was used to raise rabbits to be sold as pets or as food in Boston.

Outer Brewster with its cliffs and caves has been called one of Boston's most romantic spots.

Rainsford Island has served as the site of a hospital for infectious diseases, a quarantine station, an almshouse, and the House of Reformation for boys.

1634

An early attempt to lure settlers was William Wood's tract *New England Prospects,* published in London. Wood called Boston:

> *Very pleasant, hem'd in on the South-side with the Bay of Rox-berry, on the North-side with the Charles-river, the Marshes on the backe-side, being not halfe a quarter of a mile over; so that a little fencing will secure the Cattle from the Woolves. [The city is free from] the three great annoyances of Woolves, Rattle-snakes and Musketoes.*

Q: How many species of snakes can be found in the Boston area?
A: Actually, Wood was not totally correct. The Blue Hills are home to thirteen species of snakes, including two poisonous ones, copperheads and timber rattlers. Tourists should also note that the occasional mosquito does stray into the Boston area.

1635

The Great Colonial Hurricane blew on August 16:

> *It blew down many hundreds of trees . . . overthrew some houses, and drove ships from their anchors.*
>
> —JOHN WINTHROP

1638

The earliest recorded severe earthquake in Boston occurred on June 11. It was especially severe in the Plymouth area. Modern seismologists guess the severity as 6.0 on the Richter scale. It toppled objects and people and was followed by a less severe aftershock about half an hour later.

1663

A severe earthquake on February 5 had its epicenter in Quebec where trees were uprooted, landslides started, and courses of rivers changed, but it merely toppled chimneys and shattered dishes in Boston.

1677

The first map printed in the Massachusetts Bay Colony was William Hubbard's map of New England.

1697–98

Q: How snowy was the winter of 1697–98?
A: Called the "terriblest winter of the century," this season accumulated a reported forty-two inches of snow in Cambridge in February.

1717–18

It snowed for four straight days in February, shutting down the city for six days, exactly as it would be shut down 260 years later. Cotton Mather was astounded that the churches were closed on the Sabbath—and that cattle with ice over their eyes strayed into the ocean and drowned.

1727

A severe quake shook Boston and points north. Newbury minister Mathias Plant described aftershocks continuing for days. People claimed they smelled sulfur and thought that this proved the earthquake was the work of the devil. Plant recorded 120 aftershocks.

1750–1850

Weather historians call this one-hundred-year period a "little ice age."

1779–80

Historical testimony suggests that January 1780 may have been the coldest month since Europeans arrived in Boston.

1755

On November 18, seventeen days after a terrible earthquake at Lisbon, Portugal, killed thousands, Boston felt a major quake. A

Swans and the Swan Boats created in their image have become symbols of Boston's Public Garden.

careful account was left by Prof. John Winthrop of Harvard, grandson of Boston's founder. By accident the exact time of the shock was recorded. Winthrop had just set his clocks and had enclosed a long glass tube inside the tall case of the clock for safety. This tube was broken, stopping the clock at the exact time of the earthquake, 4:11 A.M. More than one hundred chimneys were leveled, fifteen hundred windows were shattered, and some wooden houses were destroyed.

1770

On October 20 a gale destroyed more than one hundred vessels in Massachusetts Bay, killing more than one hundred people.

1786

The 1,503-foot Charles River Bridge between Boston proper and Charlestown was the first bridge to span the Charles entirely within the city. The Charles River Bridge featured seventy-five piers, a thirty-foot-wide draw, and a pedestrian walkway with rails.

The West Boston Bridge, the fourth bridge to span the Charles River, was completed in 1793. This bridge was 3,483 feet long and cost $23,000 to build. The Galen Street Bridge at Watertown Square was built in the 1640s, followed by the Great Bridge at Harvard Square in 1662. The Longfellow Bridge from Boston to Cambridge was built in 1908, and an elevated subway line was added in 1912.

1799

In the late eighteenth century, Boston China traders introduced the ailanthus tree to the United States via Boston.

1804

On October 9 the "Snow Hurricane," a late tropical storm, struck the Northeast. It did not bring snow to Boston, but it toppled the steeple of the North Church and stripped the roof of King's Chapel. At least three people were killed.

1816

Q: Why was this year called "the Year without a Summer"?
A: Frosts were recorded in every month, and snowflakes were seen around Boston on June 8.

1830

Boston Common was declared a park, and cattle were no longer welcome to graze there.

1839

Q: Where did Longfellow get the idea for his poem "The Wreck of the Hesperus"?
A: Three December storms wrecked ninety ships and killed approximately two hundred people. Henry Wadsworth Longfellow wrote "The Wreck of the Hesperus" during these storms, perhaps borrowing the name of a schooner damaged at Rowe's Wharf and transferring it to a North Shore reef called Norman's Woe.

1851

A gale knocked over Minot's Light, a lighthouse off the Cohasset shore, killing its occupants. Tides rose to more than fifteen feet, and Boston's waterfront area was flooded.

The house sparrow was introduced into Boston and other East Coast cities from which sparrows rapidly spread throughout the country.

1872

Boston's financial district, sixty-five acres in the center of the city, burned to the ground on November 12, a little more than a year after the Great Chicago Fire. The cause of the fire remains unknown.

I saw the fire eating its way straight toward my deposits.
—OLIVER WENDELL HOLMES

The Old South and Faneuil Hall are in Boston, but they are the treasures of the country. The painful, almost gradual

*approach of the flames . . . was shared by those in distant parts
of the country who could see only by telegraph.*

—*HARPER'S WEEKLY,* 1872

1881

Q: What is the "Emerald Necklace"?

A: Frederick Law Olmsted developed his plan for the Emerald
Necklace, Boston's park system. Olmsted had already designed
a park for Boston's Fenway area. The Emerald Necklace
extends some five miles, from the Boston Common to Jamaica
Pond and Franklin Park. Olmsted articulated his six principles
of landscape alliteratively as scenery, suitability, sanitation, sub-
ordination, separation, and spaciousness.

Olmsted, who had designed New York's Central Park, fell in love
with Boston and moved to the city in 1881 after visiting his friend,
architect H. H. Richardson, in Brookline. Looking out upon a new
snowfall and a snowplow clearing the street, Olmsted is said to have
exclaimed, "This is a civilized community. I'm going to live here."

*[Jamaica Pond should be] for the most part shaded by a fine
natural forest growth to be brought out overhangingly, darken-
ing the water's edge and favoring great beauty in reflections
and flickering half-lights.*

—FREDERICK LAW OLMSTED

1888

The great storm of November 25–26 caused some forty shipwrecks
in Massachusetts Bay.

1891

The 2,165-foot-long Harvard Bridge was built to connect Boston's
Back Bay to the section of Cambridge where MIT would later be
headquartered.

1892

Landscape architect Charles Eliot was largely responsible for establishing the Metropolitan Park Commission, reorganized as the
Metropolitan District Commission in 1919.

1898

Q: How severe was the Portland Gale?

A: Almost a decade to the date after one great storm, the Portland Gale of November 26–27 wrecked nearly 150 vessels and killed more than 450 people. Winds in this storm reached 100 miles per hour.

1899

The mile-long Charles River Speedway for harness racing opened along the riverbank in Allston-Brighton.

1908

A wooden dam was built across the mouth of the Charles River, excluding the ocean's tides from the basin. A stronger masonry dam replaced the wooden structure three years later.

1911

Q: How hot was it in the summer of 1911?

A: The heat wave of 1911 began on July 1. On July 2, as the temperature neared 100, the first deaths and hospitalizations were reported. Boston's all-time high temperature of 101.6 was recorded on July 3, and the record was broken on the Fourth of July with an official reading of 103.6. On July 6 thunderstorms cooled things off briefly, but the 100+ temperatures returned on July 10 and 11. The heat wave killed more than eleven hundred people in Massachusetts in July.

1914

At Mystic Wharf in Charlestown, some one hundred monkeys escaped from their pens on the British ship *Montrose*. A crowd gathered to watch as the Chinese crew chased the monkeys all over the ship.

1919

Q: What was the Great Molasses Flood?

A: On January 15, at the corner of Foster and Commercial Streets in Boston's North End, a ninety-foot tank of molasses exploded. The sticky stuff, two million gallons of it, weighed more than fourteen thousand tons. A thirty-foot-high wave of molasses swept through the streets.

The molasses was being used by the Purity Distilling Company in munitions manufacturing (the Eighteenth Amendment had made the production and sale of rum, along with other alcoholic beverages, illegal). The company eventually had to pay more than $1 million in damages to survivors and owners of damaged property. Final casualty count of the Great Molasses Flood was 21 dead and 150 injured.

1927

On June 1 the *Boston Floating Hospital* burned to the waterline in its berth at a pier in North End Park.

Boston Common marks the start of the city's five-mile chain of parks known as the "Emerald Necklace."

After his flight across the Atlantic, a triumphant Charles Lindbergh greeted a crowd of two hundred thousand on the Boston Common.

1934

Q: How cold did it get in the winter of 1934?
A: Boston's record low temperature of 18 below zero was recorded on February 9.

1936

A crowd of 175,000 listened to Franklin Delano Roosevelt on the Boston Common during FDR's campaign for a second term.

1938

The "Great Hurricane of 1938" (hurricanes did not receive personal names until 1953) hit Boston on September 21. This storm killed some six hundred people in New England. This was New England's last category 4 storm, with winds between 130 and 155 miles per hour. The 1938 hurricane destroyed 15 percent of all New England's mature timber. Continuing the Massachusetts history of dessert disasters, the storm caused a tapioca spill in the Athol River.

1942

Q: What was Boston's worst disaster?
A: Boston's worst disaster ever was the Coconut Grove fire on the night of November 28. This disaster killed 490.

Many at the Melody Lounge of the South Boston club had planned to attend a celebration of a Boston College football victory over Holy Cross. Instead, the BC Eagles lost, 55–12.

Officially the fire was ultimately labeled "of unknown origin," but some witnesses reported that it began when sixteen-year-old busboy Stanley Tomaszweski attempted to change a light bulb hanging on a potted palm while using the light of a match.

All exits were partially or completely blocked. A revolving door jammed, four doors were locked, and two new doors that opened inward proved useless. This disaster led to the creation of new fire codes across the country, as well as to new techniques for treating burn victims.

1960

A minute after takeoff from Logan Airport on October 4, Eastern Airlines Flight 375 ingested a flock of starlings into its engines and crashed into Winthrop Bay. Three of four engines failed, and sixty-two of seventy-two people aboard were killed.

Steve Carlson, age eleven, found a six-and-a-half-foot mastodon tusk at the edge of Spy Pond in Arlington. Carbon dating established that the tusk was some forty-two thousand years old.

1974

The Army Corps of Engineers built a new and larger Charles River dam a half-mile closer to the ocean in order to reduce the likelihood of flooding. Cost of the new dam was $48 million.

1978

The blizzard of '78 dumped two to four feet of snow on the Boston area, with abnormally high tides and fifteen-foot drifts. A National Guard report called it "the most destructive storm" in Massachusetts history. Some twenty-nine people were killed as a result of the blizzard, and damage was estimated at $1 billion.

More than three thousand cars were stranded on Boston's beltway, Route 128, and Gov. Michael Dukakis banned all but emergency vehicles from all roads for six days, in this city that is proud of its capacity to deal with snow.

Three events contributed to the severity of the storm. The moon was at its closest point to earth and in a rare alignment with the earth and sun. Meanwhile, low-pressure systems from Canada and the Gulf Stream converged. The resulting blizzard began in Massachusetts on February 6 and ended more than thirty-two hours later.

1979

A crowd of four hundred thousand gathered on the Boston Common to celebrate Mass with Pope John Paul II.

Completed in 1908 and at first redundantly called the Cambridge Bridge, this 3,500-foot-span was renamed for poet Henry Wadsworth Longfellow.

1996

Commissioned by the U.S. Fish and Wildlife Service in 1981 to trap snowy owls and remove them from Logan Airport, naturalist Norman Smith by 1996 had banded and removed more than two hundred birds. Snowy owls summer in the Arctic and like to spend winters in the American Northeast. More snowy owls winter at Logan Airport than at any other location.

Now honored with a statue in front of the State House, Mary Dyer was hanged for bringing her Quaker ideas to Boston.

2

Not Our Cup of Tea

Boston's history to 1776

This Town of Boston has a history. It is not an accident, not a windmill, or a railroad station, or crossroads tavern, or an army barracks grown up by time and luck to a place of wealth; but a seat of humanity.

—RALPH WALDO EMERSON

BOSTON'S POSITION AS THE incubator of liberty was never simple or straightforward. The Puritans who founded the city had been seeking religious liberty—for themselves. Many of them, and their descendants, remembered this fact and applied the principle to others. The majority did not. The conflict between the drive for liberty and the difficulty of extending it to all has become a major theme both of Boston's history and of America's.

Boston today remains rightfully proud of its central position in the movements for the abolition of slavery and for women's right to vote. The passionate struggle over busing and the desegregation of Boston's schools shows that creating full liberty and justice for all is a complex task. Abigail Adams, wife of the second president of the United States (and the first Bostonian president), wrote about women's rights in amazingly modern terms:

Remember the ladies. Be more generous and favorable to them than your ancestors. Do not put such unlimited power in the hands of the husbands. If particular care and attention is not paid to the ladies, we are determined to foment a rebellion, and will not hold ourselves bound by any laws in which we have no voice or representation.

In the twentieth century Boston has lost its position of national leadership in many areas, though not, perhaps, in fields such as learning, literature, music, and medical care. Many Bostonians, though not all, are proud that their state was the only one to give its electoral votes to Vietnam War opponent and social liberal George McGovern rather than ill-fated Republican Richard Nixon in the 1972 presidential election.

While millions of tourists have visited Boston's Freedom Trail, it's common to hear Bostonians say, "I've never done the whole walk. I'll get around to it sometime." But most Bostonians know something about John and Samuel Adams, Paul Revere, the USS *Constitution,* and John F. Kennedy. There is another freedom trail etched in our minds. We have not yet built the end of it. Bostonians and other Americans may differ on how far it should go and which ways it should turn, but most agree that we need to keep the path we have in good repair.

1700 B.C.

Q: What is the oldest evidence of people living in the Boston area?

A: The oldest evidence of human life in Boston is Indian fish weir stakes found alongside the Charles River. These were found in 1913, when the Boylston Street subway was being dug.

CA. A.D. 1000

Q: Did Leif Erikson visit Boston before Christopher Columbus's voyage to the New World in 1492?

A: Some claim that Leif Erikson founded a land, Vinland, and built a house, Leifsbudir, on the banks of the Charles River, but scholars have doubted the evidence on which the claim was based. Every year around Columbus Day, October 12 (a Massachusetts state holiday), Bostonians hotly debate the question of which European was really the first to visit America.

1602

Bartholomew Gosnold was the first Englishman to land in Massachusetts. He discovered and named Cape Cod.

1614

Q: Who led the first whale-watch in North America?
A: Capt. John Smith was the first Englishman to sail into Boston Harbor.

We found this whalefishing a costly conclusion; we saw many and spent much time in chasing them but could not kill any.
—CAPT. JOHN SMITH

Thus in the early seventeenth century Captain Smith simultaneously laid the foundations for Melville's *Moby Dick,* demonstrated the superior intelligence of cetaceans, led the first whale-watching expedition, and did his part to save the whales.

1625

Q: Who was Boston's first settler?
A: The Reverend William Blackstone (also spelled Blaxton) settled alone by a freshwater spring on Beacon Hill to pass his time gardening and reading.

1630

In March, John Winthrop, governor of the Massachusetts Bay Company, led more than one thousand Puritans on eleven ships sailing for America. Winthrop commanded the flagship of the fleet, the *Arbella.*

The journey took three months. The Puritans landed first at Salem but found the area unsatisfactory. They moved on to Charlestown but were forced to move again to find fresh water. Finally they found it on the Shawmut Peninsula, on Beacon Hill, where William Blackstone was living.

On September 7 the Massachusetts General Court officially named Boston after the English city.

1632

Q: What was the first antismoking law?

A: Boston passed the world's first law against smoking in public:

> *Nor shall any take tobacco in any inne, or common victual house, except in a private room there, so as the master of said house nor any guest there shall take offence, under pain of 2 shillings and sixpence for every such offence.*

1634

America's first public park, the Boston Common, was created.

1635

Q: What was America's first public school and what happened to its first schoolmaster?

A: Boston citizens opened Boston Latin School, America's first public school, on April 13. Philemon Pormort was the first schoolmaster, but he took the side of accused heretic Anne Hutchinson and was forced to leave for New Hampshire in 1638.

Famous graduates of Boston Latin School include:

Cotton Mather	Charles Bulfinch
John Hancock	Ralph Waldo Emerson
Samuel Adams	George Santayana
Benjamin Franklin	Arthur Fiedler
Wendell Phillips	Leonard Bernstein

1636

Roger Williams fled to Rhode Island to avoid being sent back to England by the Puritans.

Q: How was Harvard College founded?

A: The Massachusetts General Court chartered Harvard College and appropriated £400 to get it started. The college opened in 1638 in Newtowne, later renamed Cambridge. A young clergyman named John Harvard died in 1638 and left some £1,700 to the college, which was named Harvard College by the general court in 1639.

1637

The Pequot War of 1637 began with the killing of John Oldham aboard a boat at the mouth of Narragansett Bay. Capt. John Mason and John Underhill then led a punitive expedition against the Indians, killing more than six hundred Pequots.

1638

Anne Hutchinson was tried for heresy by the general court, found guilty, excommunicated, and banished from the colony.

Q: What were the heresies that led to Anne Hutchinson's trial and banishment?

A: Hutchinson's heresies included maintaining that God spoke to her and that it was through God's grace rather than people's good works that people would achieve salvation. Hutchinson attracted crowds of up to eighty people to her house to listen to her religious commentaries and prophecies.

After her banishment, Hutchinson traveled to Rhode Island and farther to Dutch-controlled Long Island. There, she and her family were killed by Indians in 1643. John Winthrop, who had described Hutchinson as a woman of "ready wit and bold spirit," believed that her fate represented divine retribution.

1639

When the general court authorized Richard Fairbanks's tavern to be a repository of mail, America's first post office was created.

1640

The first slaves brought to New England arrived, and the general court immediately ordered them to be returned.

1641

The general court adopted America's first statute prohibiting cruelty to animals: "It is ordered by this Court that no man shall exercise any tyranny or cruelty towards any brute creatures which are usually kept for the use of man."

1642

Q: What were the provisions of America's first compulsory education law?

A: America's first compulsory education law was passed, establishing coeducational public schools in Boston and requiring that all children attend. In 1647 the court passed a law requiring that every community of fifty or more families must have a teacher.

1644

Massachusetts established the nation's first bicameral legislature, which would eventually serve as a model for the structure of the United States Congress.

Baptists were banished from Massachusetts, and Presbyterians would be banished two years later. The general court mandated that all Indians must worship God.

1645

Pilgrims sought the help of Boston Puritans against the invasion of the French.

1648

Boston's role in labor history began with the formation of the first American guild authorized to elect its own officers, the shoemakers and coopers' guild.

Q: Who was the first woman in America to be hanged as a witch?

A: Margaret Jones of Charlestown became the first American woman to be hanged as a witch. Three more women were hanged as witches in Boston.

1649

Gov. John Winthrop was buried in King's Chapel Burial Ground on today's Tremont Street.

Q: Who was the first Jew to arrive in Boston?

A: The first Jew in Boston was Solomon Franco, who had taken passage aboard a cargo ship. He was expelled twelve days later.

1650

Q: What were the "Praying Towns"?

A: John Eliot established a settlement for Indians converted to Christianity at Natick, now a western suburb of Boston. Natick achieved relative prosperity, and soon fourteen other "Praying Towns" were established around the bay.

Eliot made a tender of the everlasting salvation to that king ; but the monster entertained it with contempt and anger. . . . He took a button upon the coat of the reverend man, adding, That he cared for his gospel, just as much as he cared for that button.
—COTTON MATHER, 1702

1652

John Hull and Richard Sanderson minted America's first coins. The first design was too easy to forge or trim, so a few months later they created new coins known as "pine tree shillings." The colony had been operating on a barter system because England forbade colonies to use currency.

1655

Ann Hibbens was hanged as a witch at Boston Neck.

1656

The general court enacted an early environmental regulation. It provided that the only place butchers could dispose of "their beasts' entrails" was from a bridge in the North End.

1660

Q: Who was Mary Dyer?

A: After being expelled from Boston for her Quaker beliefs, Mary Dyer returned to Boston from Rhode Island and was hanged on Boston Common.

1674

Edward Randolph, an agent of the British crown, reported that the Bostonians were violating trade and navigation laws, defying the king's authority, coining their own money, and restricting political power to Congregationalists. Randolph recommended using troops if necessary to "reduce Massachusetts to obedience."

1675

Q: How did King Philip's War start?

A: Wampanoag sachem Metacom, son of Massasoit, who had been friendly with the early colonists, refused to submit to the authority of the colony that wanted to control the lands he considered to be his. King Philip (as he was known to the English) "determined not to live until I have no country," persuaded Nipmucs and Narragansetts to join him in a war against the Massachusetts Bay Colony.

In an action that foreshadowed the internment of Japanese Americans during World War II, the colonists sent hundreds of friendly Indians from the Praying Towns to camps on Boston Harbor islands. By the end of the war, many had died of starvation.

Some twenty-five hundred colonists and at least as many Indians were killed in King Philip's War. On Boston Common, forty Indians captured during the war were executed.

1676

King Philip was killed. His head was displayed at Plymouth, and one of his hands was awarded to the Pocasset tribesman who killed him.

1684

The old charter of Massachusetts Bay Colony was annulled as the British crown attempted to make the Bostonians more subservient.

1686

James II sent Royal Gov. Sir Edmund Andros to Boston to be governor-general of the Dominion of New England.

1688

A woman known only as Mrs. Glover was executed as a witch.

1689

Q: How did Bostonians deal with Governor Andros?

A: When the news of the Glorious Revolution—when Parliament replaced James II with William of Orange and his wife, Mary—reached Boston, Bostonians threw Governor Andros into jail, declared their allegiance to the new monarchs, and petitioned for the return of the Charter of 1629. William and Mary agreed to a compromise charter that recognized property rather than religion as qualification for voting and office-holding.

1692

Q: How did the Salem witch trials come about?

A: Elizabeth Parris, nine, and her cousin Abigail Williams, eleven, suffered fits and convulsions. Elizabeth's father, Minister Samuel Parris, unpopular and fearful of losing his job, pressured the girls to name their tormentors. They accused Tituba, a slave in the Parris household, poor and slovenly Sarah Good, and the somewhat flirtatious and irreligious Sarah Osborne.

Tituba confessed under coercion, and some 150 more people were arrested. In all, 19 were hanged.

In October Massachusetts Gov. William Phips halted further trials and declared supernatural "evidence" invalid.

1700

Catholic priests were banned in Boston.

1713

Builder William Payne erected the structure that came to be known as the Old State House. Boston's first public reading of the Declaration of Independence took place on a second-floor balcony on July 18, 1776.

Following Paul Revere's instruction, sexton Robert Newman hung two lanterns in the Old North Church steeple on April 18, 1775.

1721

Q: Why did somebody throw a firebomb into Cotton Mather's house?

A: The house of the Reverend Cotton Mather was firebombed because Mather supported Brookline physician Zabdiel Boylston, who was attempting to introduce vaccination for smallpox.

A smallpox epidemic had begun in Boston when a ship from the West Indies brought two slaves to the city who were ill with the disease. In the city of eleven thousand, close to six thousand caught the disease and more than eight hundred died.

British medical literature recognized that inoculating people with a mild form of the disease could lead to immunity. A slave in the Mather household testified that his tribe did the same. But inoculation was a risky procedure. Boylston inoculated some 250 people, and 6 of them died.

1722

Q: Where was America's first billiards parlor?
A: America's first billiards parlor was opened in Charlestown.

An Italian Jewish scholar, Judah Monis, arrived at Harvard to teach Hebrew and Old Testament studies.

1726

Hoop petticoats were banned in Boston.

1742

Peter Faneuil financed the construction of the first Faneuil Hall, designed by John Smibert, and donated it to the city. Sam Adams regularly gave speeches there advocating the overthrow of British rule. In later decades, William Lloyd Garrison spoke against slavery at Faneuil Hall, Susan B. Anthony advocated women's rights, Suzette LaFlesche spoke for Native American rights, and John F. Kennedy concluded his successful 1960 presidential campaign.

1746

The Ancient and Honorable Artillery Company, the first military company chartered in the Western Hemisphere, established its headquarters at Faneuil Hall.

1748

The Old State House was rebuilt after being destroyed by fire.

1754

The French and Indian War began.

1761

Faneuil Hall burned to the ground. The city immediately rebuilt it, financing the project through a public lottery.
    Faneuil Hall's original weathervane, a thirty-eight-pound gilded copper grasshopper designed by sculptor Shem Drowne, was retained atop the restored building.

1763

The French and Indian War was ended by the Treaty of Paris. George III turned his attention to the unruly American colonies and Parliament passed restrictive laws that included the Sugar Act, assigning the Royal Navy to patrol American waters and to try cases of smuggling.

> *[The Sugar Act] set people to thinking, in six months, more than they had done in their whole lives before.*
>
> —JAMES OTIS

Boston's population of about sixteen thousand remained steady during the 1760s while New York and Philadelphia surpassed this mark.

Boston's first sewer was dug.

1765

Parliament passed the Stamp Act, imposing special taxes on all legal and commercial documents of the colonists. Boston merchants boycotted British goods, and mobs stoned and looted the homes of Gov. Thomas Hutchinson, the local stamp agent, and the customs collector.

Q: Who first said, "Taxation without representation is tyranny"?
A: "Taxation without representation is tyranny" became a slogan of the protesters. Though some have attributed the saying to Virginian Patrick Henry, later testimony by John Adams suggests that it may have been coined by Boston lawyer James Otis in February 1761, during an eight-hour speech against the Writs of Assistance, delivered at Boston's Old State House.

> *Otis was a flame of fire. . . . Then and there the child Independence was born.*
>
> —JOHN ADAMS

Concerned Bostonians formed the Sons of Liberty to monitor the situation and to threaten reprisals. The Stamp Act was repealed in March 1766.

1767

A year after the repeal of the Stamp Act, England adopted the Townshend Acts. These imposed import duties on American goods including tea. The Sons of Liberty were in the forefront of a storm of protest.

1768

British agents boarded John Hancock's ship *Liberty*.

1770

The crown instructed Governor Bernard to dissolve the Massachusetts legislature and sent soldiers to protect customs officials.

The Boston Massacre took place on March 5. A group of Bostonians gathered at the Custom House after drinking at the Bunch of Grapes Tavern on what is now State Street. The crowd taunted a lone sentry until the noise attracted a column of Redcoats. The British troops fired on the mob, killing five people. One of those killed was a black man, Crispus Attucks. Some of the Townshend Acts were repealed later in March, but the tax on tea was retained.

1773

The Tea Act of 1773 granted tax-free status to the British East India Company.

Q: How many people took part in the Boston Tea Party, and what did they wear?

A: The Boston Tea Party took place on the night of December 16. Some fifty men dressed as Mohawk Indians boarded three British ships at Griffin's Wharf and dumped their cargoes of tea into the water while crowds cheered.

1774

Parliament responded to the Boston Tea Party with the Coercive Acts, a series of laws aimed at controlling and punishing Boston. The Boston Port Act closed Boston Harbor and imposed a blockade. Gen. Thomas Gage was made military governor.

Bostonians continued to defy the British. Some left the city to join rebel forces or to do business elsewhere. Many who remained refused to sell food or provide lodging for General Gage's troops. Colonials began to stockpile weapons and ammunition in towns such as Concord, Massachusetts.

1775

On April 18 General Gage sent seven hundred men to seize military supplies at Concord. Paul Revere and others had warned the colonists on horseback before the British arrived.

Q: Who were the other riders who alerted the colonists that the British were coming?

A: William Dawes and Dr. Samuel Prescott helped Revere alert the countryside. Prescott knew the area well, and he and Dawes may have alerted many more colonists than did the more renowned Paul Revere. Many others also rode that night.

Q: What was the name of Paul Revere's horse?

A: It was Brown Beauty.

Armed Minutemen met the British on Lexington Green on April 19. The British fired on the defiant colonists, killing eight and wounding ten. The battles of Lexington and Concord marked the opening of the American Revolution.

On June 17 the battle of Bunker Hill took place (though not on Bunker Hill). Some twenty-five hundred British soldiers succeeded in dislodging colonial troops from Breed's Hill in Charlestown. The 221-foot obelisk commemorating the battle stands on Breed's Hill.

Q: Who first said, "Don't fire until you see the whites of their eyes"?

A: Legend attributes the phrase "Don't fire until you see the whites of their eyes" to British Col. William Prescott at Breed's Hill. In fact it was already a military cliché, probably first spoken by a Prussian officer decades earlier.

George Washington arrived in Cambridge in July to take command of the colonial troops. He was appalled at both the lack of discipline (soldiers were electing their own officers) and the lack of artillery.

The winter of 1775–76 was bitterly cold, and hundreds of Boston's buildings and trees were burned for fuel. Food became scarce, and starvation was averted by donations from other colonies.

1776

Q: How did George Washington get the cannons he needed to Boston?

A: Washington had sent Gen. Henry Knox of Boston, a former bookseller, to Vermont to bring back cannons captured from the British by Ethan Allen at Fort Ticonderoga. Washington was heavily criticized for inaction while waiting for the guns. Knox succeeded in hauling more than fifty cannons over two hundred miles in three months on sleds pulled by oxen.

Washington had learned from the battle of Bunker Hill that he would need well-prepared fortifications to defeat the British. He ordered readymade units and had his army bring them rapidly, with his fifty cannons, to Dorchester Heights.

When British Gen. William Howe saw Washington's fortifications and cannons overlooking Boston Harbor on March 5, he hastily ordered his troops to evacuate Boston without a fight.

Boston's population fell from nearly twenty thousand to less than six thousand during the Revolutionary War.

John Hancock and others signed the Declaration of Independence.

Defeated by Confederate Gen. Robert E. Lee at the May 2–3, 1863, battle of Chancellorsville, Union Gen. Joseph Hooker now guards the Massachusetts State House.

3

A Melting Pot of Beans

Boston's history since 1776

> *Boston is the one place in America where wealth and knowledge of how to use it are apt to coincide.*
>
> —E. L. GODKIN, 1871

1778

Voters defeated a proposed constitution for Massachusetts, drawn up by the legislature, by a five-to-one margin, because it lacked, among other things, a bill of rights and provisions for religious freedom.

1780

Q: Who wrote the Massachusetts constitution?

A: John Adams submitted a draft of a constitution for Massachusetts. Adams's draft began with the words, "All men are born free and equal." After the constitution was approved, Massachusetts courts affirmed that it prohibited slavery. The census of 1790 indicated that there were no longer slaves held in Massachusetts.

John Hancock became the first independent governor of the state of Massachusetts.

1781

Cornwallis surrendered.

1787

After Boston merchants persuaded the legislature to revoke backing of paper money, many Massachusetts farmers were unable to pay their debts and lost farms to foreclosure. In the counties between Boston and Springfield many decided to take up arms to overthrow the Massachusetts government.

In January 1787 Daniel Shays led some twelve hundred farmers in an attack on the federal arsenal in Springfield, Massachusetts. The farmers broke ranks after four had been killed and twenty wounded. For a month they raided shops and harried the state militia. After a defeat at Petersham, Massachusetts, Shays fled to Vermont. Shays and thirteen others were condemned to death but were eventually pardoned and allowed to return to their Massachusetts homes.

1789

Unable to send their children to established all-white schools, Boston blacks set up a school of their own in the home of Prince Hall.

1795

Paul Revere organized the nation's first labor union.

1796

John Adams became the second president of the United States.

Q: Who managed the Adams farm while John Adams served as president?

A: His wife, Abigail, managed the family farm in Braintree while Adams served as delegate to the Continental Congress, then as vice president and president. Her letters to her husband are well known.

Remember the ladies. Be more generous and favorable to them than your ancestors. Do not put such unlimited power in the hands of the husbands. If particular care and attention is not paid to the ladies, we are determined to foment a rebellion, and will not hold ourselves bound by any laws in which we have no voice or representation.

—ABIGAIL ADAMS

1797

The frigate *Constitution* was launched.

1798

Paul Revere founded Massachusetts Mutual Fire Insurance Company.

The new State House, designed by Charles Bulfinch, was completed on January 11 at a cost of $133,333.33. The famous Golden Dome began as a cupola of dark wood. It was covered with copper

During the Revolutionary War, the British used the gravestones in Copp's Hill Burial Ground for musket practice.

in 1802 by Paul Revere & Sons, then gilded with 23-carat gold leaf in 1874. During World War II the dome was painted over in gray to hide it from possible air attacks.

1799

The Boston Board of Health, directed by Paul Revere, was formed with the goal of combating yellow fever.

1800

Boston's population reached twenty-five thousand.

1808

Q: Who was the first bishop of Boston?
A: The Catholic Church chose Jean Louis Anne Magdeleine Lefebvre de Cheverus to be the first bishop of Boston.

1809

The African Meeting House became Boston's first "Negro" church, a place for exchanging information as well as for holding religious services.

1810

Boston's population passed the thirty-thousand level.

1812

Q: Where did the term "gerrymander" come from?
A: Republican Gov. Elbridge Gerry rearranged congressional districts on Boston's North Shore to favor his party. Engraver Elkanah Tisdale published a drawing in the *Boston Weekly Messenger* depicting a map of the district with a dragonlike head and claws. A reader's observation that it looked more like a "Gerrymander" than a salamander created a new political term.

The term gained popular acceptance and helped to defeat Gerry in the next gubernatorial election. However, he went on to win election to higher office, serving as vice president under James Madison.

Q: How did the USS *Constitution* get its nickname?
A: The frigate gained fame and the nickname of "Old Ironsides"
in the War of 1812. In an engagement with the British frigate
Guerriere, a cannonball bounced off the *Constitution*'s hull, and
a sailor exclaimed, "Good God! Her sides are made of iron!"

A poem by Oliver Wendell Holmes helped save the *Constitution*
from being scrapped in 1828, and today the ship has seemingly
found a permanent home at a dock in Charlestown.

1820

The national census counted 43,298 Bostonians.

1822

An act establishing the city of Boston was signed by Gov. John
Brooks. City government, headed by a mayor, a board of aldermen,
and a forty-eight-member common council replaced the old town
structure. Compromise candidate John Phillips became the first
mayor, but Josiah Quincy was elected the next year.

Mayor Quincy set out at dawn every morning on horseback to
survey the city. The marketplace established by Peter Faneuil was
renamed Quincy Market in Josiah Quincy's honor.

1823

Mayor Quincy appointed Benjamin Pollard "marshal of the city" to
head the police department and act as the city's public health officer. Quincy established a team of street sweepers and ordered refuse
to be collected regularly.

Dr. John Collins Warren became president of the Massachusetts
Society for the Suppression of Intemperance. Warren persuaded the
mayor to prohibit the sale of alcohol in public places. The movement became increasingly militant with the formation of the
Massachusetts Temperance Society in 1833.

1824

John Quincy Adams was elected president.

Q: What did John Quincy Adams do after his presidency was over?
A: After the presidency, he returned to Washington as a congressman. He was threatened with censure for presenting an abolitionist petition to the Congress in 1837. In 1841 Adams successfully defended a group of slaves who had mutinied on a Spanish slave ship. He died in 1848 after collapsing while delivering a speech against the war with Mexico.

1825

The American Unitarian Association, an organization composed of individual members, was formed. During the previous two decades, numerous Congregationalist pulpits in Boston had been taken over by Universalists. In an 1819 sermon, William Ellery Channing had defined Unitarian Christianity. Unitarians favored individual moral responsibility and took a leading role in the abolitionist movement.

Nothing quieted doubt so completely as the mental calm of the Unitarian clergy. Doubts were a waste of thought. . . . Boston had solved the universe.

—HENRY ADAMS

1826

Q: Which two of America's Founding Fathers both died on the same significant day?
A: John Adams and Thomas Jefferson both died on July 4, 1826.

The Union Oyster House opened at 41 Union Street.

1831

William Lloyd Garrison founded the *Liberator,* the influential abolitionist journal.

1832

Horace Mann established the nation's first public school system. Boston's third mayor, Harrison Gray Otis, received angry letters from the governors of Virginia and Georgia demanding that he take action against William Lloyd Garrison's abolitionist publication, the *Liberator*.

Dr. Samuel Gridley Howe opened the New England Asylum for the Blind, renamed the Perkins School for the Blind in 1833 when Thomas Handasyd Perkins donated his home as headquarters for the school.

1834

Q: How did a Boston mob come to burn down a convent?

A: Anti-Catholic rioters burned down the Ursuline Convent in Charlestown. The Mount Benedict School for Girls admitted both Catholic and Protestant students. Someone, purportedly a former student of the school, wrote a pamphlet alleging that Protestant students at the school were pressured to convert to Catholicism.

Rumors spread rapidly, and on August 11 a crowd of some four thousand gathered. They threw stones through the windows and finally set the school on fire. Occupants escaped, but the school was destroyed.

1835

Q: How did William Lloyd Garrison avoid being lynched by a Boston mob?

A: A mob broke up a meeting of the Boston Female Antislavery Society and dragged William Lloyd Garrison through the streets. Garrison was arrested and jailed for his own protection after he fled to the Old State House and was given shelter by Boston Mayor Theodore Lyman Jr. Circumstantial evidence suggests that the mob was organized by some of Boston's leading merchants, who were upset by the radical views Garrison expressed in his abolitionist journal, the *Liberator*. The incident led to expressions of support for Garrison from prominent business and literary figures.

1837

As president of the Massachusetts senate, Horace Mann led the movement to establish the country's first state board of education. Mann left the legislature to serve as the board's secretary for eleven years, championing equality, nonsectarian education, and professionalism in teaching.

1841

Dorothea Dix visited a jail in East Cambridge. Appalled at the conditions, she wrote a memorandum to the state legislature. One of her complaints concerned the mixing of the mentally ill with other criminals, and her arguments led to the creation of state hospitals for the mentally ill.

Q: Who started Brook Farm?
A: George and Sophia Ripley founded the utopian community Brook Farm.

1843

The first synagogue of the Jewish community of Boston was Kahal Kadosh Ohabei Shalom (the Holy Community of Lovers of Peace).

1845

Political and economic troubles in Ireland, culminating in the Potato Famine, led to waves of immigrants arriving in Boston. In 1840, some 3,900 immigrants arrived in Boston. By 1849 the number arriving had swelled to 28,917. By 1855 there were more than 50,000 Irish living in the city.

Q: Was the Potato Famine the primary factor that drove Irish immigrants to Boston?
A: No. Politics, more than the Potato Rot of 1845, caused the immigration. English absentee landlords had long kept the

Irish tenant farmers in poverty. The Irish farms produced potatoes to feed the tenants and grains for export to profit the owners. When grain prices fell and competition from more efficient agriculture elsewhere made the Irish farms unprofitable, absentee landlords raised rents, and the Potato Famine made it impossible for tenant farmers to eat and pay rent. No longer useful to the owners, they were evicted in increasingly large numbers. Farms were converted to pasture.

1846

Q: How did the Massachusetts establishment protest against one of America's early wars?

A: The Massachusetts General Court denounced Pres. James K. Polk's declaration of war against Mexico. Many regarded the war as a grab for land and an attempt to expand the nation's territories where slavery was permitted. Governor Briggs of Massachusetts refused to commission volunteer officers for service beyond the commonwealth.

1849

Charles Sumner represented Benjamin F. Roberts and his five-year-old daughter, Sarah, in a lawsuit against a school that had denied her admission because she was black. The Massachusetts Supreme Court ruled against Roberts.

1850

The landmark Report of the Sanitary Commission was issued under the supervision of state representative Lemuel Shattuck of Boston. The report showed that Boston's rising mortality rate was associated with environmental and social factors and argued that public authority was needed to monitor and improve public health.

1854

The legislature passed a law that no child could be denied admission to a school on account of race, color, or religious opinions.

Until recently, Chinatown residents had to pass a former peepshow store-front to get to the subway station.

In May, escaped slave Anthony Burns was seized in Massachusetts under the federal Fugitive Slave Law of 1850. Attempts by out-raged citizens to free him in Boston had to be turned back by more than two thousand marines, army, and police.

1855

Boston's main drainage system was installed.

Harvey Parker opened his restaurant, later renamed the Parker House, serving meals à la carte at irregular hours.

1858

On October 11, Sen. Jefferson Davis, passing through Boston on his return from a vacation in Maine, spoke in favor of slavery and national unity at Faneuil Hall.

1860

The Reverend Theodore Parker died on May 11 in Florence, Italy. Parker was a Unitarian theologian, scholar, and reformer whose

West Roxbury congregation reached six thousand. He was indicted for sheltering fugitive slaves but was never brought to trial. Parker wrote numerous influential essays and letters, including "Letter to the People of the United States Touching the Matter of Slavery." Parker is credited with coining the famous phrase adapted by Abraham Lincoln, "Government of, by, and for the people."

On December 3, mob violence between abolitionists and anti-abolitionists broke out at a meeting at Tremont Temple. The meeting had been called by abolitionists to commemorate the first anniversary of the execution of violent abolitionist John Brown. An organized crowd of antiabolitionists tried to take over the podium, and the abolitionists retreated to a black Baptist church on Joy Street.

1862

Following the battle of Antietam, Dr. Oliver Wendell Holmes received a telegram informing him that his son, an officer in the Twentieth Massachusetts Infantry, was wounded. Holmes immediately traveled to the battlefield and searched for his son among the dead and dying. When he found him alive, Holmes supposedly inquired simply, "How are you, boy?" His son allegedly replied, "How are you, Dad?"

It was like the table of some hideous orgy left uncleared.
—OLIVER WENDELL HOLMES, DESCRIBING THE ANTIETAM BATTLEFIELD.

1863

Q: Who led the Union's first black regiment?
A: Col. Robert Gould Shaw was killed leading the Fifty-fourth Massachusetts Infantry into battle near Charleston, South Carolina. Shaw's regiment was the Union's first black regiment. Confederates buried him with his men in a mass grave, intending the act as an insult. Shaw's family viewed the burial as an honor and persuaded the Union army not to recover Shaw's body and separate it from his comrades.

Sgt. William Carney received four bullet wounds recovering the regiment's flag and became the first black American to receive the Medal of Honor.

Gen. Joseph Hooker of Massachusetts took control of the Union army in March 1863 and was outmaneuvered by Confederate Gen. Robert E. Lee at Chancellorsville two months later. An equestrian statue of Hooker stands in front of the Massachusetts State House.

Q: How did the term "hooker" originate?

A: Contrary to common belief, the word *hooker* as it has come to be applied to prostitutes did not come from General Hooker's name and was not first applied to women who followed the general's camp. The term can be traced to 1845 or earlier and may derive from a New York neighborhood known as "The Hook," from Dutch-American slang for huckster, "hoeker," or simply from the action of a prostitute taking her prospective customer's arm. During the Civil War, soldiers did refer to Washington, D.C., prostitutes as "Hooker's division."

1875

Q: Who founded the Christian Science Church?

A: Mary Baker Eddy published her book *Science and Health,* setting out her philosophy of Christian Science. Eddy wanted to return to primitive Christianity with what she considered its lost power to heal. In 1892 Eddy organized the Mother Church in Boston to oversee the worldwide network of the Church of Christ, Scientist.

1882

The Hotel Vendome at the Corner of Commonwealth Avenue and Dartmouth Street was the first public building in America to be lighted with electricity.

1893

Arthur Shurtleff, a student at the Harvard Divinity School, began the tradition of Christmas lights by putting a lighted candle in a window of his parents' home on West Cedar Street.

1897

Q: Where was America's first subway?

A: The Tremont Street Subway, America's first underground subway system, was completed on schedule and for less than the $5 million that the legislature had appropriated for its construction. On an average weekday in the 1990s, some 105,000 people pass through Park Street Station.

1912

The legislature passed important labor reforms setting the maximum workweek at fifty-four hours and requiring a minimum wage for women that would be adequate to live on. Lawrence mill owners used the shortened workweek as an excuse to cut pay, and workers at two mills went on strike, despite the fact that they were not organized. IWW organizers arrived and were jailed on fake murder charges. Some 150 workers and children were arrested.

Q: Why did the strike of 1912 become known as the Bread and Roses Strike?

A: A photo of a young girl on the picket line carrying a sign that read "We want bread and roses too" gave the strike its name.

1914

James Michael Curley was elected mayor for the first time.

1918

More than 198,000 men from Massachusetts served in World War I, and some 5,700 died.

1919

Boston police joined the American Federation of Labor (AFL) and went on strike on September 9. National Guardsmen in South Boston fired on a pro-union demonstration, killing two boys. In Scollay Square a man was killed and a woman wounded when National Guard cavalry charged into a group of demonstrators.

Gov. Calvin Coolidge, however, insisted, "There is no right to strike against public safety by anyone, anywhere, anytime." Public opinion opposed the strikers, and AFL Pres. Samuel Gompers sent the strikers back to work. Coolidge's strike-breaking success was a major factor in his rise to the White House.

Julia O'Connor led another strike in the same year, a walkout of eight thousand New England telephone operators.

1928

The first computer was developed at MIT.

1933

The Sacred Cod that hung in the State House above the Gallery of the House of Representatives was stolen and subsequently returned by student members of the *Harvard Lampoon.* The Cod, which dated from sometime before 1784, had been donated by merchant John Rowe, after whom Rowe's Wharf is named. It was Rowe who had suggested the idea of throwing tea into Boston Harbor to protest unfair taxes.

1936

The Mary Ellen McCormack project in South Boston was the first federally funded housing project in the United States.

1944

The Harvard–IBM Mark 1 Automatic Sequence Controlled Calculator, an early computer more than fifty feet long, made its debut.

1945

During World War II, some 15,000 men and women from Massachusetts died. Approximately 225,000 served.

1947

Logan Airport opened. The original airport was on Bird's Island in Boston Harbor, and arrivals had to be ferried to the mainland. The airport expanded through landfills, with runways extending to the former Apple and Governor's Islands.

1955

Q: Where did Martin Luther King Jr. receive his doctoral degree?
A: Martin Luther King received his Ph.D. from the Boston University School of Theology. King lived on Columbus Avenue in the South End.

Q: What was the subject of Martin Luther King's doctoral thesis?
A: King's thesis was "A Comparison of the Conceptions of God in the Thinking of Paul Tillich and Henry Nelson Weiman."

1960

The Boston Redevelopment Authority (BRA) demolished a neighborhood, Boston's West End. Some 130 buildings housing numerous apartments and businesses were destroyed. About seven thousand people were evicted and forced to relocate. Many of the apartments

Each day more than 100,000 people pass through Park Street Station, America's first subway stop.

had been rat-infested slums, and the destruction included the brothels, vaudeville theaters, and strip joints of Scollay Square.

The West End was replaced by huge government buildings and upscale apartments. After the fact it was generally agreed that something terrible had happened—the destruction of a community and the callous displacement of its people.

Brookline-born John F. Kennedy was elected thirty-fifth president of the United States.

1966

Boston's law banning all forms of contraception was repealed after Catholic Church leaders declared that legislators could consider birth control as a public policy rather than a moral issue.

1968

The Sacred Cod was again stolen from the State House and again returned.

1972

Q: Which state was the only one to give its electoral votes to George McGovern instead of Richard Nixon?

A: Massachusetts was the only state won by Democrat George McGovern in his presidential race against Richard Nixon. McGovern opposed the Vietnam War and supported a guaranteed annual income plan.

1974

Boston busing riots took place. In 1972 the NAACP had sued the city of Boston in federal court in an attempt to end racial segregation of schools. Judge W. Arthur Garrity decided the case in the plaintiff's favor, declaring that Boston's schools were in fact unconstitutionally segregated. The decision meant that the schools would have to be integrated by busing students from one neighborhood to another.

Busing began in September 1974. Protesters threw rocks at buses carrying African American students. Demonstrations outside Boston City Hall turned violent on several occasions, and violence forced the closing of schools in Roxbury and South Boston. A Pulitzer Prize–winning photograph by *Boston Herald* photographer Stanley Foreman showed a black lawyer being attacked by a man wielding an American flag.

1976

Q: Where did the "First Night" New Year's celebrations begin?
A: The nation's first First Night celebration, a cultural, alcohol-free alternative to traditional New Year's Eve celebrations, was held in Boston.

1981

Passage of the controversial "Proposition 2½" lowered property taxes throughout Massachusetts and resulted in a reduced credit rating for Boston, as well as less money for education and public services.

1990

The census counted 574,283 Bostonians, making Boston the nation's twentieth most populous city.

Built in 1912, Filene's and its famous basement lure hordes of bargain hunsters to Downtown Crossing.

4

Shopkeeper, Traders and Techies

Commerce from Cogan to Ponzi, from nails to Patriot missiles

The people here are a little aristocratical but—they don't trouble thereselves much about politics as money & business is their aim.
—D. R. BURDEN, LETTER, 1796

BOSTON'S EARLY SEAGOING MERCHANTS were smart, daring, ruthless, and, frequently, successful. Opportunities for wealth abounded, and many took advantage. The risks and the gains were enormous,

Some activities of the early traders were highly questionable, to say the least. Most troubling was the triangular trade that developed in sugar, rum, and slaves. The enslavement of human beings was one of the great crimes of history, and Boston, like the rest of the nation, is still struggling with its legacy.

The history of early Boston business is, to a large extent the history of the founding of many of the city's prominent families, such as the Lowells, Adamses, Perkins, and Cabots. It is also, at times, a history of ingenuity and invention.

One of the most inspiring of Boston stories is the story of how Francis Cabot Lowell did the seemingly impossible by memorizing the details of England's burgeoning textile industry in 1810 when he toured the factories without being allowed to take notes. After he established his factories, Lowell paid attention to the conditions of his workers. He has been credited with bringing modern industry and the modern corporation to America—in some ways most of today's U.S. corporations have not yet caught up to him.

In the latter half of the nineteenth century, the story of Boston business was one of losing leadership to New Yorkers, robber barons, and railroad men, although Boston investors continued to play key roles.

But science and invention helped Boston return to prominence in the twentieth century. Although New Yorkers gained control of the telephone business, Alexander Graham Bell invented it in Boston. The Polaroid camera and much early electronics and computer technology originated here. The Internet, which is rapidly changing the face of our social and cultural worlds, was hacked together largely at the Cambridge firm of Bolt, Beranek, and Newman.

The center of the computer industry has moved elsewhere, but Boston continues to lead in scientific innovations. Boston's entrepreneurs still have spunk as well as patriotism—witness the most successful microbrewery in the country, and its inspired product, Samuel Adams beer.

1635

In Boston's earliest days, before there were retail merchants or retail stores, ships bearing goods would dock in the harbor and people would board and bargain for what they wanted to use, resell, or trade.

Q: Who was Boston's first storekeeper?

A: John Cogan. Attempting to create a more orderly process and to keep prices from spiraling, the colonial government authorized one representative from each of Massachusetts's nine towns to buy goods and resell them to the public. This system failed after four months, and retail merchants began to sell merchandise. Cogan is said to have opened Boston's first retail shop.

1639

Robert Keayne was fined £200 for overcharging customers for goods such as nails, buttons, and thread. Though the fine was later reduced to £80, Keayne wrote that some had wanted to fine him

£1,000, and the Puritan court said the merchant was dishonoring God's name with his practices.

1641

After civil war in England had cut off the flow of goods from there, Gov. John Winthrop commented, "These straits set our people on work to provide fish, clapboards, plank, etc., . . . and to look out to the West Indies for a trade."

1643

Q: What was the first ship built in Boston?

A: The first ship built in Boston, the *Trial,* returned from its maiden voyage in 1643. Its first captain, Thomas Coytemore, traded barrel staves and fish for wine and sugar in the Azores, then traded wine for cotton, tobacco, and items salvaged from wrecks in the West Indies.

1645

By the city's fifteenth birthday, Boston had built fifteen wharves.

1660

Restoration of the monarchy in England helped to support a growing merchant class of Royalists who were not Puritans in Boston.

1672

Q: Who was Alice Thomas?

A: Whipped and banished from Boston for being a "common Baud" and giving her customers "opportunity to commit carnall wickedness," tavern-keeper Alice Thomas later helped pay for a protective sea wall in the harbor and was allowed to return to the city.

1673

On February 5, an unnamed rider brought America's first mail from New York to Boston via the 250-mile route that became known as the Old Boston Post Road. The trip took two weeks.

1683

Merchant John Hull had part ownership of some fourteen ships between 1670 and 1683. Such arrangements were becoming common among Boston merchants.

1687

[Merchant Samuel Shrimpton and his party] come in a Coach from Roxbury about 9 aclock or past, singing as they come, being inflamed with drink. . . . [T]hey stop and drink Healths, curse, swear, talk profanely and baudily to the great disturbance of the Town and grief of good people. Such high-handed wickedness has not been heard of before in Boston.
—SAMUEL SEWALL, DIARY

In the same year, a French traveler observed that almost every well-to-do Boston household owned at least one slave.

1698

Lord Bellomont, royal governor of Massachusetts, observed that Boston merchants owned more ships than Scotland and Ireland combined. Boston's volume of trade was quadruple that of New York.

1700

A Bostonian would seek his fortune in the bottom of hell, but a Virginian would not go four steps for it.
—FELIX DE BEAUJOUR

1736

The Saints of New England import so many Negroes hither that I fear the Colony will sometime or other be Confirmed by the name of New Guinea.
—COL. RICHARD BYRD

Q: What was the triangular trade?

A: In this period Boston merchants developed the evil but profitable practice that became known as the "triangular trade," bringing rum to Guinea to trade for slaves, then trading slaves for sugar cane in the West Indies, then bringing the sugar cane back to Boston to be turned into more rum. Boston merchants may have continued trading slaves until as late as 1850. The city also became a center of antislavery sentiment and activism.

1740

Boston had become the largest town in North America, with more than forty wharves to its credit. The shops and warehouses that had sprung up on the waterfront were beginning to spread inland, into residential areas.

Britain was at war with Spain, and Thomas Hancock, uncle and adoptive father of John Hancock, went into the business of supplying beef and pork to the British army and navy in the Caribbean. Thomas started out in the book and stationery business, expanded to trade in other merchandise, and did particularly well trading whale oil. Eventually he owned virtually all of Beacon Hill. Though Hancock owned at least one slave, there is no evidence that he took part in the slave trade.

1742

Peter Faneuil completed construction of the marketplace and hall that bear his name. Faneuil inherited much of his wealth from his merchant uncle Andrew Faneuil. Andrew had first intended to make Peter's brother Benjamin his sole heir, but Andrew had stipulated that his heir must never marry, and Benjamin was disinherited when he fell in love and disobeyed this injunction.

1753

Postmaster Benjamin Franklin placed stones to mark the miles along the Boston Post Road. The primary purpose of these milestones was to aid the accurate determination of postal charges.

1761

Faneuil Hall burned down but was rebuilt in time to serve as a meeting place for colonial dissidents whose discontent led to revolution.

1764

Thomas Hancock died, leaving his wealth and business to nephew and adopted son John Hancock.

1784

Investors including Judge John Lowell and merchants Thomas Russell and Stephen Higginson founded the Massachusetts Bank, the second bank in the newly independent nation (the Bank of North America, formed in Philadelphia, was the first).

1790

Q: How did the China trade begin?

A: The *Columbia* arrived back in Boston after a three-year voyage that marked the beginning of the China trade that would make numerous Bostonians rich during the next fifty years. The *Columbia* was financed by six investors, three from Boston and the others from Cambridge, Salem, and New York.

Although the *Columbia* was the first Boston ship to return from China, it was the fifteenth American ship to make the journey. Boston, however, was destined to take the lead in the China trade. The *Astrea,* owned by Salem merchant Elias Hasket Derby, returned from China about the same time as the *Columbia.* Bostonian Thomas Handasyd Perkins, age twenty-four, was in charge of cargo on the *Astrea.* Perkins was to become one of Boston's richest men, giving his house and his name to the Perkins School for the Blind in Watertown.

1793

A second bridge was built across the Charles River, this one linking Boston to Cambridge. The first had been a forty-two-foot-wide toll bridge, completed in 1786, to Boston's Charlestown section.

1796

The Boston ship *Otter* landed at Monterrey, California, for provisions—the first U.S. contact with the Spanish-occupied territory.

The ship was on its way to the Northwest to trade for furs to bring to China. The northwestern Indians called all American traders "Boston Men." Boston China traders laid the groundwork for the eventual statehood of California, Oregon, Washington, and later Hawaii.

1799

Elias Hasket Derby died, leaving what was said to be the largest fortune in the United States at the time.

1802

John Lowell died suddenly at the age of fifty-nine.

Q: How did John Lowell make his fortune?
A: Lowell had grown rich handling legal matters for pirates and disposing of the estates abandoned by British Loyalists after the Revolution. He left his estate to his son Francis Cabot Lowell (Harvard, class of 1773).

1805

American merchants, including Bostonians, began selling opium to China.

1808

The great number of new and elegant buildings which have been erected in this Town, within the last ten years, strike the eye with astonishment, and prove the rapid manner in which the people have been acquiring wealth.
—A VISITOR RETURNING TO BOSTON AFTER A LONG ABSENCE

1810

Recuperating from nervous exhaustion, Francis Lowell took his family to England. There he surreptitiously studied the textile mills of England's incipient industrial revolution. Prohibited from making any notes, Lowell memorized the workings of the machines. He also encountered a distant relative from Boston, Nathan Appleton, who was doing the same thing. They agreed to work together, and Lowell, who was better at understanding the machinery, continued his investigations.

1813

Lowell founded the Boston Manufacturing Company with investors Patrick Tracy Jackson, Jackson's brothers, and Nathan Appleton.

1814

Lowell and master mechanic Paul Moody opened their manufacturing plant in Waltham, nine miles west of Boston on the Charles River.

> *Lowell was no mere mechanic, enthralled by the workings of wheels and gears, spindles and looms. What he had in mind was nothing less than the prototype of the large modern corporation, the precursor of American big business. . . .*
>
> *At Waltham, Francis Cabot Lowell had put the entire textile-making process under one roof. . . . It was a pattern that would later be followed in other industries as well—Henry Ford was to carry it to its zenith—and it was the first demonstration of the great genius and promise of American industry.*
> —RUSSELL B. ADAMS JR., *THE BOSTON MONEY TREE*

1816

The first Perkins company ship to trade opium in China, the *Monkey,* arrived in China. John Perkins Cushing and brothers Robert Bennet Forbes and John Murray Forbes were active in the opium business. The voyage of the *Monkey* was so profitable that the Perkins firm sent an agent to Italy to buy opium.

Q: Who founded the first savings bank in America?
A: John Lowell (son of Judge John Lowell), Russell Sturgis, and Joseph Coolidge were among the investors who opened the Provident Institution for Savings in the Town of Boston, the first incorporated savings bank in the country.

1817

Francis Cabot Lowell died at age forty-two. Patrick Jackson and Nathan Appleton took over. Boston newspapers nicknamed Appleton "The Great Manufacturer."

1818

Q: How did trust funds originate?

A: Trustees of the new Massachusetts General Hospital formed the Massachusetts Hospital Life Insurance Company to raise money. The plan was to create a new type of savings bank, accepting money in trust and paying interest. The plan to raise money for the hospital led to the creation of the first trust funds.

1820

The Boston Manufacturing Company sold $260,000 worth of cotton cloth.

1822

Demand for cotton cloth exceeded the supply, so Jackson and Appleton found a site north of Boston with water power for a new factory. They created the Merrimack Manufacturing Company. Imitators followed. The site became the town of Lowell.

Following Lowell's vision, Appleton and Kirk Boott established a community with an eye toward creating pleasant conditions for their workers, mostly girls from New England farms. Harriet Robinson, who worked in Lowell in the 1840s, would eventually write in her book *Loom and Spindle, or Life Among the Early Mill Girls,* that Lowell's system assumed that "corporations should have souls."

Men working in the mills received a weekly salary of up to eight dollars. Women were paid about half the wages of the men.

1827

Q: Where is the Bunker Hill Monument?

A: The Bunker Hill Monument, commemorating the 1775 battle of the Revolutionary War, actually stands on Breed's Hill in Charlestown. Intended to celebrate the battle's fiftieth anniversary, the monument was not actually completed until 1841. But it did inspire the creation of one of America's first commercial railroads (a nearly concurrent project in Baltimore opened first).

Designed by Boston architect Solomon Willard (and assisted by Alexander Parris, the designer of Quincy Market), the monument is a granite obelisk that rises 221 feet and contains 294 steps.

Getting enough granite from Quincy to Charlestown was a problem solved by Boston engineer Gridley Bryant, who suggested a railway for horse-drawn carts. Thomas H. Perkins and Amos Lawrence were among the project organizers. The Granite Railway Company delivered granite to other Boston projects. In 1870 its granite rails were replaced with iron.

1835

While he was speculating in real estate, Patrick Tracy Jackson bought Pemberton Hill, the eastern peak of the Trimountain. The hill was leveled and carted away under the supervision of farmer Asa G. Sheldon and with the muscle power of mostly Irish workers. Peter Faneuil's mansion was torn down, and Jackson sold twenty-five building lots in what would become Pemberton Square.

Three rail lines serving Boston opened in 1835. These included the Boston and Lowell Railroad, financed by Perkins and Jackson as well as Amos and Abbot Lawrence, John Amory Lowell, and others, connecting the textile mills to the north with the city. This railroad replaced the no longer adequate Middlesex Canal. The Boston and Providence and Boston and Worcester lines opened at about the same time. Soon afterward, another line connected Boston and Providence, and by 1841 Boston was connected by rail to Albany, New York.

1839

The first railway commuter line, operating between Dedham and Boston, opened.

1841

Eben March founded the Jordan Marsh Company, which became Boston's biggest department store before it was absorbed by Macy's in 1997.

1845

The Boston people are certainly the only Community who understand Rail Roads. At the present time they have more money than they know what to do with.
                                    —J. J. STACKPOLE, RAILWAY ANALYST

Boston investors were disappointed that Massachusetts rails had not displaced the Hudson River as the best way to bring goods to the East Coast. By 1845, however, some $130 million had been invested in all U.S. railroads, and $30 million of it came from Boston.

1847

Q: What Bostonian failed to buy most of the land that would become Chicago?

A: On a western trip to inspect railroads, John Forbes passed up an historic opportunity. While staying in Chicago, then a town of fifteen thousand, he was offered the chance to buy much of the city's downtown area for $1.25 an acre.

1848

Boston had seven rail terminals by 1848. Some eighty stations were in operation within a fifteen-mile radius, and some 20 percent of Boston businessmen commuted by rail.

George Higginson, along with his wife's cousin John C. Lee, formed the stock brokerage and investment firm that became Lee, Higginson, and Company.

1850

The home of Lewis and Harriet Hayden became a stop on the Underground Railroad—a safe house for runaway slaves.

1854

A choir that included students from the Perkins School for the Blind sang at the funeral of Thomas Handasyd Perkins.

Q: How did the capital of Kansas come to be named after a Bostonian?

A: Amos Adams Lawrence, son of textile giant Amos Lawrence and himself an active businessman, was a founder of the New England Emigrant Aid Company, organized with the aim of bringing Kansas into the Union as a free state. The organization financed some thirteen hundred emigrants to Kansas and provided them with weapons, shipped in boxes labeled "Books." Citizens of Wakarusa, Kansas, changed the name of their city to Lawrence, and Amos Lawrence donated another $10,000 to help found the University of Kansas.

1855

John Forbes raised $1 million to connect the Great Western Railroad to Niagara Falls, completing the rail link between Chicago and the East Coast.

1856

Q: Who created the Boston Symphony Orchestra?

A: Unable to concentrate on business, Henry Lee Higginson, son of Lee, Higginson, and Company founder George Higginson, went to Europe for four years, mostly to study music, to his father's disgust. Henry Higginson, however, returned to make fortunate investments in the Calumet and Hecla Copper Mine and, reluctantly, to join Lee, Higginson, and Company. Immensely successful in spite of himself, Higginson created and supported the Boston Symphony Orchestra in 1881.

1857

In 1849, the swampy wetland of Back Bay, running west from Boston Common parallel to the Charles River, had been declared a

Work on Boston's Central Artery Project, known as the "Big Dig," will enter its second decade in 2001.

health hazard, and a committee had been set up to deal with it. Real estate development, rather than public health, was probably the true motivation behind this process.

In 1857 an ambitious development plan was approved, involving filling the swamp and building the boulevard that is now Commonwealth Avenue. The state would finance the plan through the sale of lots for private homes.

Trains thirty-five cars long, loaded with landfill materials, arrived in Back Bay every forty-five minutes throughout the night. Among those who moved into Back Bay were Isabella Stewart Gardner and her new husband and railroad man Charles Francis Adams. Adams and his brother, John Quincy Adams II, formed the Riverbank Development Company to fill more land along the Charles. The two brothers developed Bay State Road.

1860

The textile mills of Waltham, Lowell, and Lawrence vastly increased the market for cotton, unwittingly adding to the agrarian South's attachment to the status quo, including slavery. So the industrial revolution in Massachusetts was a factor in the coming civil war.

1862

Thomas Perkins Cushing died, leaving behind a fortune approaching $2 million.

1864

Charles Russell Lowell, grandson of Patrick Tracy Jackson and cousin of the textile Lowells, had graduated first in his class at Harvard in 1854. He had quickly become the protégé of China trader and railroad man John Murray Forbes. But when the Civil War broke out, Lowell was commissioned a captain in the Union army. In 1864 he was killed in battle.

I hope you have outgrown all foolish ambition and are now content to become a "useful citizen." Don't grow rich; if you once begin, you will find it much more difficult to become a useful citizen. The useful citizen is a mighty unpretending hero. But we are not going to have a country very long unless such heroism is developed.
          —CHARLES RUSSELL LOWELL, LETTER TO HIS FRIEND HENRY
          LEE HIGGINSON SHORTLY BEFORE LOWELL'S DEATH

1868

Q: What was the Credit Mobilier scandal?

A: Union Pacific stockholder Jim Fisk went to court to challenge the activities of Credit Mobilier, the complex financing company that was at the heart of the effort to build a transcontinental railroad. The railroad was completed in 1869, but the scandal brought down the company's key financial figures, Bostonians Oakes and Oliver Ames.

1870

John Murray Forbes of Boston had almost succeeded in linking the East and West Coasts with his own company, the Burlington and Missouri River Railroad. But in 1870 Forbes discovered that some of his directors were profiting from sweetheart deals with their own construction company, much as had happened with Credit Mobilier.

Forbes put a stop to the double-dealing, bringing in his cousin Charles E. Perkins to help and eventually to run the company. By 1890 the reorganized Chicago, Burlington, and Quincy Railroad, run by Bostonians, was one of the largest in the country with more than five thousand miles of track.

1872

The Great Fire of November 9, 1872, destroyed much of Boston's financial district.

I have been thoroughly cured of my insane desire to turn hundreds to thousands, thousands to millions, and so on ad infinitum, and shall hope to live in the future, not for myself only but for others, especially the poor and needy.
—AUGUSTUS HEMENWAY, BOSTON MERCHANT AND
OWNER OF A CUBAN SUGAR PLANTATION

1874

On Beacon Hill, the state legislature made Massachusetts the first state to limit the mandatory workday to ten hours.

1875

Q: What was the Calumet and Hecla Copper Mine?

A: Alexander Agassiz and Quincy Adams Shaw were instrumental in establishing the Calumet and Hecla Copper Mine in Michigan. By 1875 the company was controlled by some eight hundred stockholders, mostly from Boston. The mine would yield fabulous dividends for the rest of the century, and to have been in on the enterprise from the beginning became a symbol of social prestige in Boston as well as a source of wealth.

1876

Q: Where was the telephone invented?

A: In a rented room on Court Street in Boston on March 10, Alexander Graham Bell, tinkerer and speech teacher of deaf children, spoke to his assistant, Thomas Watson, using his new invention: "Mr. Watson, come here. I want you." Bell had been granted a patent three days before.

Bell and two backers, Gardiner Greene Hubbard and Thomas Sanders, parents of two of Bell's speech students, tried to sell the patent to New Yorker William Vanderbilt's Western Union Company, but Western Union turned the deal down. Sanders, Hubbard, and Bell then formed the New England Telephone Company and the Bell Telephone Company.

1879

William Forbes, son of John Murray Forbes, saw the telephone's potential and provided the needed capital. Forbes became president of the new National Bell Telephone Company in 1879.

Western Union sued for patent infringement and began setting up its own telephone systems. But another New Yorker, Jay Gould, was gunning for Vanderbilt and set up his own company, American Union Telegraph. Gould started to buy up local Bell systems. It appeared that National Bell could not prevail against the New Yorkers' superior capital.

Gould was winning his battle against Vanderbilt, so in November 1879, Vanderbilt sold his telephone holdings to National Bell.

Gould really had been more interested in beating Vanderbilt than in cornering the telephone business. Satisfied with taking Vanderbilt's place at Western Union, Gould left the telephone business to National Bell.

American Bell was now a Boston company with a monopoly on providing local telephone service within cities. Its biggest shareholders were William Forbes and his brother Malcolm; Lee, Higginson, and Company; and Henry Lee Higginson.

1883

Q: How did Bostonians start General Electric, and how did the company come to be based in New York?

A: Maine-born Lynn, Massachusetts, shoe manufacturer Charles A. Coffin joined with Profs. Edwin J. Houston and Elihu Thomson to form the Thomson-Houston Electric Company. Nine years later Thomas-Houston merged with Schenectady, New York, company Edison General Electric to form the General Electric Company. Though New Englander Coffin was G.E.'s first president, and investors included Bostonians Henry Lee Higginson and Thomas Jefferson Coolidge, New Yorker J. P. Morgan tipped the balance of G.E. power toward the bigger city.

1884

Charles Francis Adams Jr. became president of the Union Pacific Railroad, moved its headquarters from New York to Boston, and attempted to straighten out the railroad's affairs. But the stock market crash of 1890 increased the company's debts, and Adams had to turn to New Yorker Jay Gould to rescue the railroad.

1885

National Bell's exclusive telephone rights would expire in 1894. A strategy of high pricing had meant slower expansion of service than might have been possible otherwise.

Q: How did AT&T come to be based in New York?

A: The Massachusetts legislature refused William Forbes's request to issue additional stock to raise money for expansion to intercity service. So Bell's directors created a new subsidiary in New York and named it American Telephone and Telegraph, or AT&T.

Back in 1870, Bostonian Andrew Preston had been impressed when Cape Cod captain Lorenzo D. Baker told him how he'd picked up 160 bunches of bananas from Jamaica for fourteen cents a bunch and sold them in Jersey City for more than two dollars a bunch. For the next fifteen years Baker kept acquiring bananas, and Preston sold them for him. In 1885 the Cape Codder and the Bostonian formed the Boston Fruit Company.

1890

By 1890, Godfrey Lowell Cabot had become America's fourth largest producer of carbon black, used in such products as ink, shoe polish, and paint. By 1902 Cabot was moderately rich, earning an income of $30,000 a year. Then the automobile came along, requiring as much as six pounds of carbon black for each tire. Cabot's annual income reached $500,000 by about 1925.

1899

The Boston Fruit Company merged with a New Orleans–based banana supplier to form the United Fruit Company.

Rival shoe machinery companies, under the leadership of future Supreme Court Justice Louis Brandeis, combined to form the United Shoe Machinery Corporation. One of the key companies in the merger was the Consolidated Hand Lasting Machine Company, a company based on an ingenious invention devised by former Lynn shoe factory employee Jan Matzeliger, a black man from Dutch Guiana.

South Station, Boston's major railroad station and the world's largest at the start of the twentieth century, opened its doors to passengers.

1900

James Jackson Storrow Jr. became a partner at the old Boston brokerage firm of Lee, Higginson, and Company. Storrow's father had been a patent law genius who defended Bell's telephone patents against marauding New Yorkers Vanderbilt, Gould, and others. When Storrow joined Lee, Higginson the firm was doing 95 percent of its business selling safe railroad bonds to friends and relatives. The company employed only two salesmen. Storrow hired many more and moved the company into other, though still conservative, investments. But Storrow was destined to accomplish more.

1901

King C. Gillette invented the safety razor and built his Gillette Razor Company plant in South Boston.

1909

Q: Who started Filene's basement?
A: Edward Filene opened Filene's Automatic Bargain Basement in a space below ground level on Washington Street. His unique pricing plan was to mark down items that didn't sell immediately, 25 percent after twelve days, 50 percent after eighteen days, and 75 percent after twenty-four days. Crowds began to gather before opening time to get a jump on bargains. The store became a Boston institution and a tourist attraction.

1910

James Jackson Storrow Jr. became chairman of a five-man committee charged with saving a floundering General Motors Corporation. Storrow succeeded by raising money, cutting costs, and hiring good men including Walter P. Chrysler and Charles W. Nash.

Storrow also found time for public service. He served on the Boston School Committee and helped to reform it and promoted recreational development on the Boston bank of the Charles River. In 1909 he ran for mayor of Boston and lost, though he spent $103,000, more than double the expenses of his opponent, John F. "Honey Fitz" Fitzgerald, grandfather of John F. Kennedy.

After Storrow's death, the commuter highway along the Boston bank of the Charles River was named Storrow Drive in his honor.

1912

Textile workers in Lawrence went on strike after manufacturers cut their wages in response to legislation limiting the workweek to fifty-four hours. Two were killed and several hundred arrested before owners agreed to the workers' demands.

1914

John "Honey Fitz" Fitzgerald was dismayed by his daughter Rose's marriage to the twenty-six-year-old president of the Columbia Trust Company, Joseph P. Kennedy.

During his years at Harvard, Joe Kennedy had made $5,000 operating a sightseeing bus business. Kennedy worked during the war years as assistant manager of a Quincy shipyard.

1915

A tower added to Boston's Custom House turned the 1847 building into Boston's first skyscraper.

1917

In 1917 Joe Kennedy became a trustee of the Massachusetts Electrical Company and after the war was put in charge of brokerage firm Hayden, Stone, and Company's Boston office. He bought a string of movie theaters and started a studio that turned out B movies. Eventually, Joe Kennedy moved to New York, but he maintained a base in Boston and sent his sons—Joseph Jr., John, Robert, and Edward—to Harvard.

Also in 1917, the Cape Cod Canal was opened to shipping between Boston and New York. Such a canal had been suggested as early as 1676, and in 1776 the Massachusetts legislature appointed a committee to look into the idea. In 1883 the Cape Cod Ship Canal Company began to dig but soon abandoned the project. Work was resumed in 1909 after a charter had been granted to the Boston, Cape Cod, and New York Canal Company.

1919

Q: How did the "Ponzi Scheme" get its name?

A: Charles Ponzi, who had arrived in Boston from Italy in 1903, set up an office in Boston after knocking around North America and spending some months in prison in Montreal and Atlanta. Back in Boston, Ponzi came up with a plan to exchange currency for international postal reply coupons, an idea that theoretically could generate some profits but would be difficult or impossible to develop into a major enterprise.

Ponzi promised investors a 50 percent return on their money and quickly generated a large volume of business. He paid off the earliest investors with money from the next wave, generating even more enthusiasm. Ponzi was so successful that he bought real estate, a controlling share of a small bank, a suburban home, and a macaroni company.

When the press began to question his activities, some investors asked for their money. But the publicity brought in more investment, and for a time he was able to continue paying the doubters with newly invested cash.

When the scheme finally collapsed, Ponzi was sentenced to five years in prison. His name has become synonymous with the pyramid scheme.

1922

Swedish con man Ivar Kreuger convinced Lee, Higginson, and Company to invest in his International Match Corporation. Kreuger claimed to be dealing in government-granted monopolies on match manufacture. He claimed that diplomatic considerations made secrecy essential. In the next ten years Lee, Higginson sold some $150 million worth of Kreuger's stock to investors. In March 1932, Lee, Higginson executives accompanied Krueger to Paris, intending to examine his books. Krueger shot himself in the heart before a scheduled meeting.

Lee, Higginson was forced to close sixteen branch offices and reorganize. The firm kept offices open in Boston, Chicago, and

The good times in Boston's Combat Zone have pretty much ended, but exotic dancing continues at the Glass Slipper.

New York, but the damage was irreparable. The company was forced to close its doors.

1923

The Boston Airport opened.

1924

Q: What were the first mutual funds?

A: Small investors in Boston created the Massachusetts Investors Trust to pool their funds and allow for diversified investment. Others quickly copied the innovation, and the funds became known as Boston Funds. These were in fact the first mutual funds.

1925

Boston's American Appliance Company, formed to manufacture refrigerators, acquired the rights to a new kind of radio tube and changed its name to the Raytheon Manufacturing Company. The new tubes enabled radios to dispense with large batteries and run by plugging into household electricity supplies. Raytheon would later manufacture Patriot missiles that played a key role in the 1992 Gulf War between the United States and Iraq.

1930

According to Mayor Michael Curley, some thirty thousand Bostonians were unemployed.

1933

On December 5, Prohibition was repealed, three days after women had stormed the State House, some demanding the same tavern privileges as men, others demanding the continuation of Prohibition. Boston's December 5 celebration of the end of Prohibition rivaled the revelry that had greeted the end of World War I.

1935

The American House, Boston's first hotel to have an elevator and the first to employ black waiters, closed its doors.

1937

[In Boston there is] little evidence of frenzied pursuit of expansion and grandiose development. There is far more concentration

upon the maintenance and perfection of what already exists. . . .
Boston . . . gladly turns over the exuberance of pioneering to
other sections of the country.
—DONALD HOLBROOK, INVESTMENT MANAGER

Edwin H. Land, on leave from Harvard before getting his bachelor's degree, established the Polaroid Corporation to market a filter intended to cut down the glare of automobile headlights.

1944

Q: What gave Edwin Land the idea for the Polaroid camera?

A: While shooting snapshots of his family, Edwin Land was asked when the pictures would be ready by his impatient daughter. Within six months Land had invented instant photography. His Polaroid cameras went on sale in time for Christmas in 1948.

1946

American Research and Development Corporation (ARD), formed to supply venture capital to enterprises developing new technology, opened for business. The Massachusetts Institute of Technology (MIT) and the John Hancock Mutual Life Insurance Company were among ARD's investors.

Industrial Electronics Laboratory spun off Tracerlab, Inc., to supply radioactive isotopes to hospitals, universities, and industries for a variety of new uses. ARD invested $150,000. Tracerlab annual sales reached $10 million within five years.

1947

Residents staged a sit-down strike on the sidewalks of Beacon Hill to prevent the removal of the old brick sidewalks. The demonstration was successful.

1950

The census showed that the greater Boston metropolitan area was home to 2,505,797, with 766,386 living in Boston proper.

1952

David Bakalar and his brother Leo started Transitron Electronics Corporation with about $1 million. In seven years the company was worth $150 million.

1955

By the mid 1950s, some forty high-tech companies had built their headquarters on Route 128, the beltway that forms a semicircle around the port of Boston. Before 1948 the beltway had been a country road of chicken and pig farms. By 1951 the highway was nearly complete.

Much of the industrial development of Route 128 was carried out by the real estate firm Cabot, Cabot and Forbes. F. Murray Forbes had hired Gerald W. Blakely, son of an MIT professor, after hearing about Blakely's vision of building garden-style industrial parks.

The whole secret of Route 128 was the proximity of MIT.
—GERALD W. BLAKELY

By the mid 1960s, more than six hundred businesses were headquartered along Route 128, and Gerald Blakely had become president of Cabot, Cabot, and Forbes.

1956

The Boston Airport was renamed after World War I Lt. Gen. Edward L. Logan.

1957

With help from ARD, Kenneth Olsen and Harlan Anderson started Digital Equipment Corporation, which introduced its own computer in 1960. ARD's seventy-thousand-dollar investment reached a value of more than $300 million in the 1960s.

Shanghai-born Boston University graduate Gerald Tsai Jr., working for Fidelity Fund president Edward C. Johnson II, launched his

This elegant pedestrian walkway helps shuttle shoppers to and from the posh Copley Place Mall.

creation, the Fidelity Capital Fund. Tsai favored young, risky companies such as Polaroid and Xerox.

1963

The fifty-two-story Prudential Center was completed, facilitated by legislation that provided tax concessions to the Prudential Insurance Company and strengthened the Boston Redevelopment Authority.

1966

Q: Why did Gerald Tsai move to New York?

A: Edward Johnson II had chosen his son, Edward III ("Ned"), rather than Gerald Tsai to succeed him as chairman of Fidelity, so Tsai moved to New York where he created the Manhattan Fund. Tsai was not as spectacularly successful with the new fund, and he retired from mutual fund management with a tidy fortune, just in time to miss the market's late-'60s tumble.

1969

A "People Before Highways" march to Boston Common helped to scuttle plans for the building of a massive Southwest Expressway through Boston.

Meanwhile, in September, another then little-noticed highway was getting its start in Boston. The first interface message processor, or IMP, was shipped via Logan Airport from Cambridge computer firm Bolt, Beranek, and Newman (BB&N) to the University of California at Santa Barbara to initiate the Information Superhighway, or Internet. BB&N scientist Frank Heart headed the project after BB&N won the bidding on a proposal from the U.S. Department of Defense's Advanced Research Projects Agency (ARPA), an office originally created in response to the Soviet Union's launching of the first space satellite, *Sputnik.*

1970

The U.S. Census showed that more than two thousand people commuted to work in Boston from Rhode Island and more than fifteen hundred commuted from New Hampshire.

Paradise appears on an unexpected streetcorner in Cambridge.

1972

Bolt, Beranek, and Newman (BB&N) engineer Ray Tomlinson developed the first program for E-mail at the Cambridge computer firm. Tomlinson also devised the bulk of the E-mail address system that was adopted, after much debate, using the form x@y.com.

1985

Jim Koch's Boston Beer Company sold its first twenty-five cases of Samuel Adams beer. By 1994 Boston Beer had become the tenth largest brewery in the United States with $133 million in sales. Koch started the company with $100,000 of his own money and $140,000 in loans.

1990

Raytheon developed the Patriot missiles used during the Gulf War to intercept missiles fired by Iraq, after the United States intervened to repel the Iraqi occupation of Kuwait.

1991

The multibillion-dollar Central Artery-Tunnel project, known as the "Big Dig," began under Mayor Ray Flynn. The project, far from completion as of 1999, is meant to create a third tunnel under Boston Harbor and to result in Boston's Central Artery traversing the city underground. The Big Dig is scheduled to produce 3.7 miles of tunnel, 2.3 miles of bridges, and 1.5 miles of surface connections.

1992

Only two sex-industry businesses remained in Boston's "Combat Zone," down from thirty-nine in 1977, due to suppression by the city's licensing board during the 1980s.

1994

Boston Duck Tours opened for business with four amphibious vehicles called "ducks." By 1997, Andrew Wilson had twelve ducks operating. In 1994, some three hundred thousand people took

Since Boston's financial district burned in 1872, it has been rebuilt and refurbished.

"duck tours" of Boston, visiting landmarks along the city's streets and then viewing others from the Charles River.

1995

A crowd of three thousand turned out to cheer Red Sox baseball legend Ted Williams at the dedication of the Ted Williams Tunnel, the third tunnel under Boston Harbor.

1996

Pasha Roberts won the MIT fifty-thousand-dollar entrepreneurship competition. Roberts raised $600,000 and founded Webline Communications Corpation after his business plan won the competition's thirty-thousand-dollar first prize. Entrants in the nine-year-old competition have founded more than thirty companies and have raised more than $43 million in capital. Altogether, MIT graduates and faculty founded some four thousand businesses, generating more than $230 billion in annual sales in 1994 alone.

The State House dome was built in 1798, gilded in 1874, and temporarily painted gray during World War II.

5

Beacon Hill Beauties and Beasts

The good, the bad, and the ugly in Boston politics

No allegation of municipal corruption has ever been made against any Boston official.
—BOSTON MAYOR FREDERICK O. PRINCE, 1880

LARGER-THAN-LIFE HEROES and scoundrels have populated Boston's political scene from the start. Many have been both at once.

Founder and first governor John Winthrop can be seen either way. Certainly he was a great and successful leader. He was always an autocrat, and he was harsh and vindictive toward Anne Hutchinson, whom he hounded out of the colony for heresy. But Winthrop had visionary and humane moments as well—his discourse titled "A Modell of Christian Charity," composed aboard the vessel *Arbella* before the colonists landed at Massachusetts Bay, is unique as a statement of purpose for the founding of a city.

> [W]e must be knit together, in this work, as one man. We must entertain each other in brotherly affection. We must be willing to abridge ourselves of our superfluities, for the

supply of others' necessities. We must uphold a familiar commerce together in all meekness, gentleness, patience, and liberality. We must delight in each other; make others' condition our own; rejoice together, mourn together, labor and suffer together, always having before our eyes our commission and community in the work, as members of the same body. . . . For we must consider that we shall be as a City upon a hill. The eyes of all people are upon us.

Centuries later came the prototype of Boston's political hero-villain, Mayor James Michael Curley. Curley built and spent and cared about his people and his city. He also went to jail twice and appears to have been a master of contract corruption. A novel titled *The Last Hurrah* and the movie made from it have helped to preserve Curley's legend.

John F. Fitzgerald, "Honey Fitz," was another Boston legend. He set standards of corruption, but his grandson, John F. Kennedy, became a widely admired legend in his own right as president and as victim of an assassin's bullet. The Kennedy clan, as is well known, has gone on to exemplify much of the best and worst in American public life. Sen. Ted Kennedy has been admired by many for his leadership in health care and other areas—but he has been unable to keep himself, his cousins, and his nephews from becoming embroiled in sordid scandals. Senator Kennedy's late-night accident at Chappaquiddick Island and his failure to seek help promptly cost campaign worker Mary Jo Kopechne her life. It likely kept Ted Kennedy from pursuing the presidency and so altered the course of American history.

The Kennedys were not the only Boston scoundrels. One Boston mayor had to pay to cover up an affair with a cousin of his wife that began when the girl was eleven years old. Governor's councilor Dan Coakley was impeached and convicted after a lifetime of corruption. The chairman of the commission that built the parking garage under Boston Common was convicted of bribery in the late 1950s, and in 1964 Massachusetts speaker of the house John L. Thompson died before he could be tried on thirty-three counts of corruption.

In Boston, politics has been a lucrative game for some of its participants and a spectator sport followed with passion by the public. It's also a long-running soap opera of heroes and villains, old families and recent immigrants, cynics and idealists.

1630

John Winthrop, first governor and spiritual leader of the colonists, kept extensive journals and wrote sermons expressing a sense of history and destiny for the Puritan colony of Boston.

1643

The Massachusetts General Court (still the official name of the state legislature) made the first law against election fraud, establishing a substantial fine "if any freeman shall put in more than one paper or beane for the choyce of any officer."

1703

Queen Anne of England requested that the Massachusetts General Court pay the royal governor an annual salary. The Bostonians instead voted Governor Dudley a temporary grant of £500. The royal governor's salary thus became one symbol of the conflict of wills between the American colonies and the British crown.

1747

The Old State House, formerly known as the Town House, was rebuilt after burning down for a second time. The general court met at this site from 1659 until 1798.

1767

Samuel Adams, member of the Massachusetts General Court, leader of the Sons of Liberty, and spokesman for the Boston Town Meeting, sponsored construction of the legislature's first public galleries. Opening the legislature to public view could be seen as an enhancement of democracy, or it could be regarded as a more pragmatic step to enlist the public in an effort to intimidate legislators loyal to England.

1779

On September 1, a constitutional convention was held at the First Church in Cambridge, Harvard Square. Of the 293 delegates, 4 would later become chief justices of the Massachusetts Supreme

Judicial Court, and 7 would later be governors of the state. Still, John Adams called the meeting "a chaos of absurd sentiments concerning government."

1780

The first general court under the new Massachusetts constitution convened at the Old State House in Boston. John Hancock was sworn in as the state's first independent governor.

1806

In a closely contested race for governor, illegible and misspelled ballots were at issue for weeks. The race was between Caleb Strong and James Sullivan, but the general court had to establish rules governing how to count ballots that may have said "Stoon" or "Sullvn." Fearing charges of corruption and confident that their party could control the government through the legislature, the Republican legislature gave the victory to Federalist Caleb Strong, with a Republican as lieutenant governor. In those early days in the politics of the republic, the party known as Republican sympathized with France and political progressiveness, while the Federalists leaned toward England and conservatism.

1810

Federalists raised Boston's representation in the state legislature from six to forty-two. Republicans charged that this was done by counting inhabitants of other towns, Harvard students, prisoners, and aliens as well as double-counting some voters to swell the voting lists.

1823

Q: Who was known as "the Great Mayor"?

A: Mayor Josiah Quincy, Boston's second mayor, modernized the city. He was reelected five times and has been called "the Great Mayor." Quincy reorganized the city's health department, fire department, and correctional institutions, improving conditions both for prisoners and for the poor. He inspected his city

on horseback every morning, created a street-cleaning department, and even urged double-parked wagons to move along.

*The great duty of the mayor of such a city as this is to identify
himself, absolutely and exclusively, with its character and interests.*
—Josiah Quincy

1863

John "Honey Fitz" Fitzgerald, grandfather of John F. Kennedy, was
born in Boston's Irish North End.

Q: What were some of the early nicknames of Honey Fitz and his
followers?

A: A man of many nicknames, Johnny Fitz was so fond of saying
"Dear old North End" that his supporters later became
known as "Dearos." His opponents early on gave him the
name of "Fitzblarney."

1866

Gov. John Albion Andrew retired from the State House, exhausted
after governing during the Civil War. Andrew urged Lincoln to
sign the Emancipation Proclamation and was instrumental in creating Massachusetts's "colored regiments."

*Everyone remembers the energy with which he pursued the plan
of employing colored troops, till he at last obtained permission
from the War Department. . . . But, though consenting to
receive their services, the government refused to give these men
a soldier's pay, and offered them a smaller sum, such as was
paid to stevedores and cooks. This they unanimously refused to
receive, and so went without pay for more than a year. The
Governor summoned the Massachusetts Legislature in extra ses-
sion, and procured an act to be passed to pay them the full
amount from the State treasury. . . . But these brave fellows
refused to take it, saying, "We will wait till the United States
chooses to pay us our just dues." The Governor, though a sweet-
tempered man, was capable of righteous indignation, and on*

*this occasion it burst all limits. He appealed to the War
Department, to the Attorney-general, and at last to the President. . . . The War Department at last gave way, and the colored men were made equal with the whites.*
—JAMES FREEMAN CLARKE, "JOHN ALBION ANDREW"
(EXCERPTED IN *THE MANY VOICES OF BOSTON*)

1869

Thomas Edison received his first patent. It was for an automatic vote-counting machine that he expected would soon be adopted by legislatures everywhere. It was not.

1892

Johnny Fitz, JFK's grandfather, took to politics. He joined every club and got to know every voter in the North End. The newspapers gave him another nickname, the North End Napoleon. In 1892 at age twenty-nine he was elected to the Boston Common Council and then ran for state senate. He had the good luck to run against an enemy of Martin Lomasney, known as the Mahatma of Ward 8, and Lomasney's support helped Fitzgerald win easily.

1894

After just one term in the state legislature, Fitzgerald ran for U.S. Congress and won a nasty contest against incumbent Joseph O'Neil. Ballot boxes were stuffed and stolen on both sides.

Johnny Fitz was the only Catholic in Congress during the first of his three terms. National office wasn't his goal—he was waiting for a chance to be mayor of Boston.

He acquired a weekly newspaper and made it a journal of Irish-American happenings. The *Republic* never had much readership, but it grew steadily as a moderately subtle way for advertisers to give Honey Fitz money.

1905

Boston's Democratic Party bosses chose city clerk Edward Donovan to run for mayor, but Honey Fitz challenged him in the primary. Fitzgerald ran a more aggressive and energetic campaign than anyone had ever run before. He employed the first political motorcade. He averaged ten speeches a night and gave thirty-five the night before the election. Because Martin Lomasney opposed him, Fitzgerald was trounced in Ward 8, but he still pulled out a close primary election and went on to defeat easily a split Republican Party.

Fitzgerald's administration was marked by unprecedented graft and patronage. The city overpaid for coal, cement, and land. New offices such as city dermatologist were created for friends and supporters. But Fitzgerald's energy matched his abuse of power. He is said to have attended 1,200 dinners, 1,500 dances, 200 picnics, and 1,000 meetings, and made 3,000 speeches.

1907

The Democrats were split, and Republican George Hibbard defeated Honey Fitz for mayor by promising to "clean up the mess."

1909

The 1909 campaign was a classic. Voters were tired of the colorless reformer Hibbard, and Republicans united around wealthy and distinguished James Jackson Storrow. Storrow had served on the Boston School Committee, and he had saved General Motors from possible bankruptcy.

Q: How did Honey Fitz acquire a theme song?
A: Curley and Lomasney supported Fitzgerald in an expensive and arduous fight. A week before the election, at a rally for Johnny Fitz, the band finished its songs before Fitzgerald arrived at the podium and started to play "Sweet Adeline" to fill the time. Fitzgerald reached the podium and began singing, and everyone stopped to listen. "Sweet Adeline" became his theme song, and Honey Fitz became his most enduring nickname.

The night before the election Honey Fitz spoke at thirty-five rallies and sang "Sweet Adeline" from a taxi rooftop. Storrow spent $103,000, more than double what Fitzgerald spent. But Fitzgerald won, 47,177 to 45,775.

During his second term, Honey Fitz built the City Hall Annex, the City Point Aquarium, the High School of Commerce, and the Franklin Park Zoo. Graft and patronage continued in the unrestrained fashion Fitzgerald had inaugurated during his previous term. Honey Fitz had promised not to run again, and James Michael Curley declared his candidacy for mayor. But Honey Fitz changed his mind and announced that he would challenge Curley. Curley told reporters that he was preparing three speeches: "Graft, Ancient and Modern," "Great Lovers from Cleopatra to Toodles," and "Libertines: From Henry VIII to the Present Day."

Q: Who was "Toodles?"

A: "Toodles" Ryan was a hostess at the Ferncroft Inn in Newburyport. Honey Fitz would later insist that he had never done more with Toodles than a casual kiss at a party, with his wife present. But after Curley had delivered speech number one, on graft, Fitzgerald dropped out of the race, citing ill health. He never won another election.

Honey Fitz lived long enough to see his grandson, John Fitzgerald Kennedy, win election to the United States Congress in 1946.

1917

Andrew James Peters defeated James Michael Curley in the race for mayor when Martin Lomasney and Honey Fitz outmaneuvered Curley by entering two Irish candidates to take votes away from Curley. Peters had previously served four terms in Congress. As mayor, he let the bosses who had helped elect him run City Hall, and he was never aware of the rampant bribery that went on. Peters also mismanaged the police strike of 1919 then resented Gov. Calvin Coolidge for stepping in, calling out the state guard, and suppressing the strike.

Q: Who was Starr Faithfull?

A: Peters was also implicated in a lurid scandal. He had an affair with Starr Faithfull, a cousin of his wife, begun in 1918 when Starr was just eleven years old. In 1926, when she was nineteen, Starr told her mother about the affair, and when Peters returned from a cruise, he had to pay a large settlement to the Faithfull family to keep the matter quiet.

Starr committed suicide in 1931. Her diaries were found but later destroyed. A possible connection with Andrew James Peters was mentioned in the newspapers, but investigators refused to comment. Peters continued to deny everything. The truth was widely known, but it was never reported in the press.

1930

Vice cop Oliver B. Garrett surrendered to *Boston Post* crime reporter Lawrence R. Goldberg and gave him a detailed, exclusive story. Garrett had made a fortune in graft from Boston-area speakeasies. One of his neatest tricks was to raid clubs that were paying him off and have their liquor poured down the sink—the clubs were equipped with special sinks that caught and saved the valuable stuff.

During his career, Garrett owned racehorses and a dairy farm. Clubs bought their milk from Garrett, and it was rumored that he developed a liquor home-delivery business.

Finally, Garrett was demoted to street duty and filed a pension claim. During investigation of the claim, many of his other activities were uncovered. He disappeared and for five months became the focus of a nationwide manhunt until he surrendered to Goldberg.

1933

Q: Who was Martin Lomasney?

A: Martin Lomasney, the Mahatma of Ward 8, died in 1933. Born in 1859, Lomasney worked as a bootblack and lamplighter before becoming a city health inspector and founding the Hendricks Club, which became the base of his political power. The name of the club came from Cleveland's vice president, Thomas Hendricks, because he had made a speech in favor of the Irish.

Lomasney's control of the voting lists in Ward 8 made him one of the most powerful men in Boston. He was known as a master of the technique of recruiting "mattress" voters—people who stayed in lodging houses to establish their residence in his district on April 1, when the voting lists were determined.

The great mass of people are interested in only three things—food, clothing, and shelter. A politician in a district such as mine sees to it that his people get these things. If he does, he hasn't got to worry about their loyalty and support.

—MARTIN LOMASNEY

Lomasney served many years in the legislature but does not seem to have been interested in higher office or in enriching himself. He did, however, maintain a real estate business and often sold property to the city for public buildings.

Q: Who was the first woman to serve in an American president's cabinet?

A: Frances Perkins, born in Boston in 1880 and raised in Worcester, became the first woman to serve in the cabinet of a U.S. president when Franklin Roosevelt appointed her secretary of labor in 1933. She was one of only two cabinet members to serve during all four of FDR's terms. Accomplishments included creation of the Civilian Conservation Corps, enactment of a federal minimum wage and limits on the workweek, and child labor laws. Her department drafted the Social Security Act and the Fair Labor Standards Act.

1941

Governor's councilor Dan Coakley was impeached in the Massachusetts house of representatives and convicted in the senate after a long career of bribery and blackmail.

In his early years Coakley worked as teamster, bartender, reporter, boxing referee, and conductor for the Cambridge Street Railway Company. He lost his job with the railway after he was caught stealing fares.

Coakley taught himself law, passed the bar, and opened a law office where for a time he specialized in suing his old employer over

*City Hall Plaza and Government Center have replaced Boston's West End
Neighborhood and Scollar Square.*

railway accidents. He supported Honey Fitz Fitzgerald for mayor
of Boston in 1905 and was rewarded with the post of Parks Com-
missioner after Honey Fitz was elected.

In 1914 Honey Fitz's enemy, James Michael Curley, had been
elected mayor, and Coakley became friendly with Curley. He became
even more friendly with district attorneys Joseph Pelletier of Suffolk
County and William Corcoran of Middlesex County. It became
widely known that a word from Coakley could stop a prosecution.

The trio of Coakley and the two district attorneys expanded
their activities to blackmailing rich Bostonians who had been
caught—or maneuvered into—embarrassing situations. Septuage-
narian Edmund Barbour paid Coakley more than $300,000 after he
was discovered with a woman some fifty years his junior. Coakley
even shook down visiting movie moguls after a wild party for Fatty
Arbuckle at the Copley Plaza Hotel.

Powerful Godfrey Lowell Cabot, treasurer of the priggish New
England Watch and Ward Society, went after Coakley and his
friends. After six years of investigations, charges, and countercharges,

during which Cabot was brought to trial and acquitted for having documents stolen from Coakley's office, Cabot finally succeeded in having Coakley, Pelletier, and Corcoran disbarred. In 1924, Coakley and Corcoran faced criminal charges. Pelletier committed suicide to avoid a trial. Coakley and Corcoran were found not guilty on all counts.

In 1928 Coakley reached an undisclosed understanding with the IRS regarding $4 million in unpaid taxes. He also ran for mayor of Boston, finishing fourth in a field of ten. His primary purpose was accomplished though, when he helped to defeat Curley's candidate.

In 1930 Honey Fitz ran for mayor against Yankee Joseph Ely. Curley was now supporting former enemy Honey Fitz, so Coakley worked for Ely. During this election Coakley did a famous series of radio broadcasts attacking Curley on radio station WEEI.

After Ely won the mayor's race, Coakley grew powerful again. He won election to the governor's council, which at that time had substantial power in dealing with the governor. With numerous endorsements, Coakley petitioned for readmission to the bar, but his petition was denied.

Curley was elected governor in 1934 and somehow the governor and the powerful governor's councilor became friends again. Governor Curley pardoned numerous criminals during his term on the basis of petitions brought by Coakley.

Q: Who pardoned Raymond Patriarca and why?

A: Joseph "Chowderhead" Hurley succeeded Curley as governor, and the stream of pardons increased. In 1938, at Coakley's behest, Hurley pardoned Raymond Patriarca after he had served eighty-four days of a sentence for armed robbery. Coakley's petition on Patriarca's behalf misrepresented the future Mafia capo's age as twenty-two when he was really thirty and included endorsements from three priests. One had been lied to, one had never agreed to endorse Patriarca, and one was a made-up name and did not exist.

When Republican Leverett Saltonstall became governor, he and house speaker Christian Herter sponsored investigations into

Coakley's activities. Coakley was impeached on fourteen counts of bribery and sale of pardons. By a vote of thirty-three to six Coakley was found guilty and removed from office.

The next year, at age seventy-six, Coakley entered the race for U.S. Senate but soon dropped out. He maintained a suite at the Parker House, a townhouse in Brighton, and a country home in Buzzard's Bay. He died on Cape Cod at age eighty-six, still threatening to write his autobiography.

1948

Democrats took full control of the State House for the first time. Truman's election helped Massachusetts Democrats win the state's house of representatives and all six executive offices, led by Gov.-elect Paul Dever. Tip O'Neill, a state legislator from Cambridge, became the first Democrat to serve as speaker of the Massachusetts house of representatives.

1950

The legislature passed a bill allowing women to serve on juries for the first time, and Governor Dever signed it into law. In 1946 a referendum had approved the measure, but the legislature had rejected it.

1956

Q: What was James Michael Curley's response to the novel *The Last Hurrah?*

A: Edwin O'Connor published *The Last Hurrah,* a novel based on the life of James Michael Curley. Curley at first threatened to sue but ended up congratulating the author.

Born to poverty in 1874, Curley got a job delivering groceries when he was fifteen and stayed at it for eight years. At the same time he was educating himself, getting to know everyone on his routes, and chairing picnics, outings, and church suppers.

In 1898 a politician known as "One-armed Peter" Whalen picked Curley to run for Boston Common Council against the organization of ward boss "Pea Jacket" Maguire. Curley received several hundred more votes than his opponent, but Pea Jacket's friends tampered with the ballot boxes and Curley lost.

The following year Curley ran again, but this time he recruited enough street fighters to control the polls. After numerous street brawls in the week before the election, Curley won a decisive victory. It was a minor office, but at twenty-six Curley became the new boss of Ward 17.

Q: How did Curley make political capital out of a term in jail?

A: In 1903, after one term in the state legislature, Curley suffered a setback. He was caught taking a civil service exam on behalf of one of his workers and sentenced to sixty days in the Charles Street Jail. In the future he would plant people in his audiences to ask about this jail term, just so he could answer, "I did it for a friend." While in jail, Curley was elected to Boston's Board of Aldermen.

Although his goal was the mayor's office, Curley conceded the post to Honey Fitz Kennedy in 1909 and ran a race that nobody expected him to win—for U.S. Congress against the incumbent, Bill McNary. It was Curley's first campaign outside of Ward 17, and he turned out to be such an effective showman that he won the race and served two terms in Congress.

In 1913 it was Curley's time to run for mayor. He ran a whirlwind campaign, promising to clean up City Hall and to provide schools, playgrounds, parks, and jobs, and he was swept into office.

Once elected, Curley opened City Hall to all and saw some two hundred people a day. His construction program was unprecedented. The subway was extended, new schools and streets were built, as well as hospitals, parks, and playgrounds. To pay for it all he borrowed and raised taxes, with much of the cost coming from the pockets of Boston's Yankee upper class.

[A] percentage of the contractors' fees would always find its way into Curley's pocket. . . . By the end of his first term he had altered the face of the city; by the end of his fourth term, the tax rate had quintupled.
—FRANCIS RUSSELL, *THE KNAVE OF BOSTON AND OTHER AMBIGUOUS MASSACHUSETTS CHARACTERS*

Q: What was the nickname of Curley's new home?

A: In the middle of his first term as mayor, Curley built himself a mansion overlooking Jamaica Pond. It became known as "the House with Shamrock Shutters." The house was valued at some $75,000, and Curley's salary was $10,000 a year. He would later claim he'd made the money through a stock market tip. A rumor, likely well founded, spread to the effect that Curley had not had to pay the contractor.

Curley lost the mayor's office in 1917 to a campaign orchestrated by Martin Lomasney and members of the business community, but he won it back in 1921 in one of the nastiest contests in Boston history.

Q: What dirty tricks did Curley use against his opponent in 1921?

A: Curley employed numerous dirty tricks against gentlemanly opponent George R. Murphy. Curley sent out campaign workers dressed as priests to spread a baseless rumor that Murphy was divorcing his wife to marry a sixteen-year-old girl. He also sent workers into Catholic neighborhoods to pose as Baptists and pretend to campaign for Murphy. At the last minute a "Personal Appeal to Women Voters" from Curley's wife, Mary, helped swing votes, and Curley won, 74,200 to 71,180.

Curley managed a neat trick at the 1932 Democratic National Convention. Excluded from the Massachusetts delegation, which supported Al Smith, Curley turned up as a member of the Puerto Rican delegation and voted for Franklin Delano Roosevelt.

Curley visited twenty-three states campaigning for FDR. He hoped to be appointed secretary of the navy, but he was informed that post was not available and that he might be considered as ambassador to Italy. When he got to see FDR, the president offered him the post of ambassador to Poland instead, commenting that it was an interesting place. Curley is said to have replied, "If it is such a goddamn interesting place, why don't you resign the presidency and take it yourself?"

Curley's third term as mayor was a more reckless version of his first two terms. His public works projects provided vital jobs during the depression. But Curley's appointment of his friend Edmund Dolan to the office of treasurer was rash.

Dolan was legal owner of Curley's ninety-three-foot yacht, *Maicaway.* Dolan directed the Mohawk Packing Company, which provided meat to city institutions at one-third more than the going rate. Dolan also ran the Legal Securities Corporation, which bought and sold bonds for the city, collecting commissions on each transaction. Dolan was eventually sentenced to two and a half years in prison, and Curley was required to pay back some $42,000 to the city treasury.

During his third term, Curley also got into a fistfight with the chairman of the Democratic State Committee at the studios of radio station WNAC.

In 1934 Curley was elected governor, and he brought his special combination of populism and corruption to bear on state government. Just before he took the oath of office, he took a swing at departing governor Joseph Ely, and a brawl ensued in the State House. During his first year he spent more than $85,000 on taxis, dinners, lunches, and the like for himself and his guests. In the winter he took his entire staff to Florida.

Curley lost the next four elections, but in 1942 at age sixty-seven he ran for Congress again. He had recently become involved with James Fuller's Engineers Group Inc., a shady organization claiming to broker deals between manufacturers seeking war contracts and government agencies. Fuller made Curley president of the company, though he appears to have done little and he resigned before the congressional election.

After an investigation of the Engineers Group, Curley was indicted for mail fraud. His trial was postponed so he could run for mayor in 1945. He won the election handily, but two months later he was convicted of mail fraud. His appeals took two years, but in the end he was sentenced to from six to eighteen months in prison. President Truman pardoned him after five months.

Q: In addition to *The Last Hurrah,* what other books were written about Curley during his lifetime?

A: With Curley's cooperation, reporter Joseph Dinneen wrote his biography, titled *The Purple Shamrock.* Dinneen acknowledged,

"There wasn't a contract award that didn't have a cut for Curley," but he argued that the good Curley did justified his practices. Curley proudly gave away autographed copies to his guests at City Hall.

With two versions of his life already in print, Curley collaborated with Honey Fitz biographer John Cutler to produce another "auto-biography," titled *I'd Do It Again.* Curley died in 1958.

1958

The legislature established the Massachusetts Parking Authority in an effort to end controversy and scandal over the proposed parking garage to be built beneath Boston Common. MPA got the job done, but its first chairman, George L. Brady, was convicted in a bribery scheme. Brady was sent to prison after hiding in New Jersey for several years.

1964

Massachusetts house speaker John F. Thompson, a Democrat and a graduate of Boston University, was named in thirty-three indict-ments for bribery and conspiracy. Thompson died in 1965 of acute alcoholism before the charges could be resolved.

1970

Sen. Edward M. "Ted" Kennedy's driver's license was revoked in Boston on May 18. The hearing examiner concluded that Kennedy had been speeding on the night of July 18, 1969, when he drove off the Dyke Bridge in Chappaquiddick, Martha's Vineyard, Massachu-setts. Mary Jo Kopechne, a worker in Robert Kennedy's presidential campaign the previous year, was drowned in the accident. Ted Kennedy did not report the accident until the next day. He testified that he dived several times in an unsuccessful effort to rescue Kopechne. Kennedy received a suspended sentence for leaving the scene of an accident. He was reelected to the Senate in 1970, but the accident at Chappaquiddick was a major factor in his decision not to run for the presidency in 1972.

The granite Ether Monument was erected in Boston Common in 1868 to celebrate the world's first successful use of anesthesia at Massachusetts General Hospital.

6

Saint Elsewhere

Boston's institutions of science, culture, and the humanities

BOSTON'S CULTURAL, HUMANITARIAN, AND scientific institutions represent perhaps the city's truest current claim to greatness.

I once stood on a Boston street corner arguing the relative merits of Boston versus New York with a prominent novelist. He carried the day in areas such as restaurants, publishing, theater, the United Nations. I had to argue that Boston does pretty well for its size. The quality of Boston's university presses and old publishing houses like Little, Brown and Houghton-Mifflin can stand up against Knopf; Farrar, Straus, and Giroux; and other examples of New York's best.

We began to consider art museums, and I had to agree that New York has more excellent ones. But Boston's Museum of Fine Arts, Isabella Stewart Gardner Museum, Fogg, and Busch-Reisinger Museums stack up well against New York's Metropolitan, Guggenheim, the Museum of Modern Art (MOMA), and Frick.

But then the momentum began to shift. Boston's Massachusetts General Hospital, Beth Israel, Deaconess, Brigham and Women's, Joslin Clinic, and more seemed to swamp Montefiore, Mount Sinai, and Albert Einstein. Perhaps it was an illusion, for the quality of medical care is not so easily quantifiable. But certainly it was no longer necessary to argue that for a small city, Boston does all right. Boston is a leader in this field.

Boston's orchestra and its universities stood up even better. The Arboretum is at least as good as New York's excellent botanical gardens. Boston's zoos fail the test, but the Boston Public Library and Harvard's Widener Library do not.

When John Adams wrote in the state constitution, "It shall be the duty of legislators and magistrates, in all future periods, to cherish the interests of literature and the sciences, and all seminaries of them—to encourage private societies and public institutions . . . to countenance and inculcate the principles of humanity and general benevolence . . . sincerity, good humor . . . and generous sentiments among the people," he was reflecting more than a desire to mold the city's character. He was emphasizing that Boston's cultural institutions should be emblematic of the city's pride. Years later, this sentiment was borne out by Mark Twain, who pointed out, "In Boston they ask, 'How much does he know?' In New York, 'How much is he worth?' In Philadelphia, 'Who were his parents?'"

The Boston Public Library

1854

Joshua Bates, an English banker who had grown up in Boston, gave the city's new public library project a gift of $50,000. The Boston Public Library was the country's first significant free municipal library. In its early years the library was inadequately housed on Mason Street and then on Boylston Street.

1860

After world-famous Boston theologian and abolitionist Theodore Parker's death on May 10, his sixteen-thousand-volume library became part of the Boston Public Library collection.

1868

Justin Winsor became director of the Boston Public Library. He was responsible for creating branch libraries that brought books to people who otherwise would not have access to them.

1880

Boston obtained a parcel of land in the Back Bay for the Boston Public Library.

1887

Q: Who designed the new Boston Public Library—and how much did it cost?

A: The city commissioned the firm of McKim, Mead, and White to provide the design for the new Boston Public Library. The original commission was to be $400,000—but the ultimate cost was $2.5 million. Charles McKim's Renaissance Revival design influenced American architecture for decades, though the library building when it opened was likened to the city morgue by the *Boston Globe*.

1895

The new main building of the Boston Public Library opened at Copley Square in Back Bay.

Q: What was the nickname given to the new Boston Public Library building in 1895?

A: Its ornate yet functional design earned the nickname "the palace of the people."

Free to All.
—ENGRAVING ABOVE THE DARTMOUTH STREET ENTRANCE OF THE BOSTON PUBLIC LIBRARY

This lion welcomes visitors and their imaginations at the entrance to the old wing of the Boston Public Library in Copley Square.

1971

Architect Philip Johnson provided the library with a major addition. A major new facade and main entrance on Boylston Street matched the old building in size and dignity, but there was no relationship in the design between the old building and the new, which was connected on the inside by a labyrinth of awkward, serpentine corridors.

1985

Arthur Curley became director of the Boston Public Library.

1997

The Boston Public Library had twenty-five branches throughout the city. It maintained sixty-five miles of bookshelves, housing some 6.1 million books, second only to New York among the country's public libraries.

The Boston Symphony Orchestra

1881

Henry Lee Higginson, son of Lee, Higginson, and Company founder George Higginson, made several trips to Europe, mostly to study music, to his father's disgust. After distinguished service during the Civil War, Henry Higginson unenthusiastically joined the family investment firm and made fortunate investments in the Calumet and Hecla Copper Mine. Immensely successful in spite of himself, Higginson created the Boston Symphony Orchestra in 1881.

1882

Q: Who was the Boston Symphony Orchestra's first conductor?
A: Under its first conductor, George Henschel, the Boston Symphony Orchestra played twenty concerts in its first season. It played twenty-six in its second season, and total attendance rose from 83,359 to 111,775.

1884

Wilhelm Gericke became BSO conductor. Under Gericke, many excellent musicians were lured from Europe, and a series of popular concerts—soon given the nickname Pops—was held.

1893

From stockholders (who never profited), Higginson raised $400,000 to build a symphony hall. McKim, Mead and White, architects of the Boston Public Library, were retained. Symphony Hall's inaugural concert was performed on October 15, 1900.

1914

The orchestra's total deficit up to this time, paid for by Henry Lee Higginson, exceeded $900,000.

In my eyes the requisites . . . were these: to leave the choice and care of the musicians, the choice and care of the music, the

rehearsals and direction of the Orchestra, to the conductor, giving him every power possible; to leave to an able manager the business affairs of the enterprise; and on my part, to pay the bills . . . and always to remember that we were seeking high art and not money; art came first, then the good of the public, and the money must be an after consideration.
        —HENRY LEE HIGGINSON, SPEAKING TO THE BSO IN 1914

1918

Q: Which conductor of the BSO was arrested during his tenure?
A: Near the end of World War I, distinguished BSO conductor Dr. Karl Muck was arrested and interned as an enemy alien.

1920

A group of thirty-six BSO musicians supported unionist concertmaster Frederic Fradkin by going on strike when Fradkin was fired for breach of contract.

1923

African-American tenor Roland Hayes sang with the BSO.

1930

The BSO played Sergei Prokofiev's Symphony no. 4 in its world premiere.

Arthur Fiedler became conductor of the Boston Pops Orchestra.

1939

The Hatch Shell was built in the Esplanade area of the Charles River and became the outdoor home of the Boston Pops Orchestra.

1946

The BSO played Aaron Copland's Symphony no. 3 in its world premiere.

1949

Q: Which Leonard Bernstein symphony had its debut with the Boston Symphony?

A: The BSO played Leonard Bernstein's Symphony no. 2, *The Age of Anxiety,* in its world premiere.

1952

Doriot Anthony Dwyer became the BSO's first woman member when she was engaged as the orchestra's first flute.

1972

During a performance of Olivier Messiaen's *Et Exspecto Resurrectionem Mortuorum,* a sixty-inch gong imported from New York shook Symphony Hall with what might have been its highest decibel level ever.

1976

John Cage's *Renga with Apartment House 1776* debuted on September 30, commissioned by the National Endowment for the Arts. The piece consisted of two separate compositions played simultaneously.

1995

Keith Lockhart, age thirty-five, became only the third conductor in the 110-year history of the Boston Pops Orchestra, replacing John Williams, age sixty-three, who in 1980 succeeded legendary conductor Arthur Fiedler.

1996

George Walker of the BSO won the Pulitzer Prize for his composition "Lilacs," written for voice and orchestra. Walker was the first black musician to receive a Pulitzer Prize.

1998

A new contract effective September 30 was initiated to raise the weekly pay of BSO musicians from $1,545 in 1998 to $1,835 in 2001.

Harvard College

1636

The general court appropriated £400 to establish a college.

[The Court] agreed to give £400 towards a schoale or colledge, whereof £200 to bee paid the next yeare, and £200 when the worke is finished, and the next Court to appoint wheare and what building.

1637

Newtowne, later renamed Cambridge, was chosen as the site for the "colledge."

Q: What alternate site was considered for the future Harvard College?
A: A three-hundred-acre farm between Salem and Marblehead was rejected as a site for Harvard.

1638

John Harvard, an assistant pastor, died of tuberculosis and left half his estate, some £700, to the new college. The next year the general court renamed the school in his honor.

1650

The general court established the president and fellows of Harvard College. This group of seven, known as "The Corporation," consisted of the president, five fellows, and a treasurer, and has continued in the same form through the 1990s. The president and fellows of Harvard College represent the oldest corporation in North America.

1764

Harvard Hall, Harvard's first library, burned, destroying the entire collection of books. All the books that John Harvard had bequeathed to the college were lost except one, *The Christian Warfare,* which had been taken out illegally by a student.

1780

Harvard was called a university by John Adams in the Massachusetts constitution.

Q: When was the Harvard Medical School opened?
A: Harvard Medical School, the first such institution in America, was established in 1781.

1817

The Harvard Law School was established.

1819

The Harvard Divinity School opened.

1877

John Amory Lowell stepped down as a fellow of Harvard College after serving for forty years.

1879

Elizabeth Cabot Cary Agassiz, granddaughter of merchant Thomas Handasyd Perkins and wife of scientist Louis Agassiz, created the Society for the Collegiate Instruction of Women, which became Radcliffe College.

1882

Daniel Chester French sculpted the statue of John Harvard that stands (or rather, sits) in Harvard Yard.

Q: Did French base his sculpture on a painting of John Harvard?
A: Since no likeness of John Harvard exists, French used Sherman Hoar, a member of the Harvard class of 1882, as his model.

The inscription on French's sculpture states incorrectly that John Harvard founded the college and that the college was founded in 1638.

1903

Harvard Stadium, designed by the firm of McKim, Mead, and White, with fifty-five thousand seats, became the world's first massive structure of reinforced concrete.

1913

Harvard's Winthrop House and Kirkland House were built. Harvard's houses serve as dormitories for underclassmen and centers of college life.

1926

The Harvard Business School was built on the Allston side of the Charles River.

1929–30

Harvard's Dunster House and Eliot House opened in Cambridge.

1965

When Paul Codman Cabot retired as treasurer of Harvard, the value of Harvard's investments had passed the $1 billion mark.

1969

On April 9 a group of students, including members of Students for a Democratic Society (SDS), seized an administration building in Harvard Yard and demanded student participation in establishing the department of Afro-American Studies and the abolition of ROTC. Harvard president Nathan Pusey called in police to end the students' occupation of the building. A two-week strike by students and faculty ensued, ending with the university's accepting the student demands.

The Massachusetts Institute of Technology

1845

Q: What brought the founder of MIT to Boston?

A: While on a trip to New England's White Mountains, Virginia geologist William Barton Rogers met Bostonian Emma Savage.

He married her four years later and moved to Boston with her after another four years. A brother, Henry Darwin Rogers, also a geologist, had drawn up a plan for a technical school that he hoped might be affiliated with Boston's Lowell Institute. The Lowell Institute rejected the plan, but William Barton Rogers used it as the basis for the Massachusetts Institute of Technology.

1861

William Rogers's efforts led to the passage of "An Act to Incorporate the Massachusetts Institute of Technology," signed by Gov. John A. Andrew on April 10.

1865

Q: How many students were in MIT's first class?

A: On February 20 the school opened with fifteen students, including a Forbes and a Cabot. The following year the university's first building, designed by William G. Preston, was completed on Berkeley Street between Boylston and Newbury Streets.

The Charles River campus of MIT has been the site of many of the world's most brilliant discoveries and most startling pranks and practical jokes.

1869

MIT's first chemistry professor, Charles W. Eliot, became president of Harvard. Merger of the two universities was discussed and rejected, as it would be twice more before 1925.

1916

MIT moved across the Charles River to its current campus in Cambridge. The Cambridge complex of buildings was designed by W. Welles Bosworth. The new campus was made possible largely through gifts from T. Coleman duPont (MIT class of 1884), who gave $.5 million in 1911, and a series of gifts from George Eastman of Rochester, New York, totaling some $20 million. Eastman had been impressed by MIT graduates who had come to Rochester to work for Eastman-Kodak.

1925

MIT professor Vannevar Bush was a major player in the founding of the Raytheon Manufacturing Company, one of the earliest in a long series of high-tech businesses that sprang up in the MIT-Harvard-Route 128-Boston orbit.

1928

Police found a cow on the roof of an MIT dormitory.

1941

Burlesque star Sally Rand was "kidnapped" by MIT students on her way to a Harvard dance and was named "Associate Professor of Entertainment Engineering" at MIT.

1979

MIT biologist Howard Green developed a method for growing large amounts of human skin quickly.

In the same year, the huge plastic steer from the front of a Saugus, Massachusetts, restaurant mysteriously appeared at the top of the great dome of MIT's Barker Engineering Laboratory.

1991

The MIT Museum and the *Journal of Irreproducible Results* sponsored the first annual Ig Nobel Prize ceremony. Thomas Kyle of MIT won the physics prize for his paper describing administratium, the heaviest element known to man. According to Kyle's paper, which Kyle claimed not to have written but merely to have signed his name to, the administratium atom consists of 1 neutron, 8 assistant neutrons, 35 vice neutrons, and 256 assistant vice neutrons. Four actual Nobel Prize laureates attended the ceremony, disguised with Groucho Marx eyebrows, noses, and glasses.

1994

A full-size replica police cruiser with blue lights flashing was found at the top of the Great Dome of MIT's Barker Engineering Laboratory.

Tufts University, Boston College, Boston University, Northeastern University, Simmons College, and Brandeis University

1852

Tufts College was incorporated on twenty acres of land that had been donated by Medford farmer and brickmaker Charles Tufts. In the 1890s Tufts Medical and Dental Schools were established in Boston to be near the city's major teaching hospitals.

1863

The Reverend John McElroy, a Jesuit born in Ireland, founded Boston College. Clothier Andrew Carney, partner of one of Boston University's founders and founder himself of Carney Hospital, provided much financial backing. Boston College was in Boston's South End for fifty years until it moved to its current site at Chestnut Hill.

1869

Q: Who founded Boston University?
A: Lee Claflin, a tanner and boot manufacturer from Hopkinton; Isaac Rich, a Boston fish peddler originally from Wellfleet

(Cape Cod); and clothing manufacturer Jacob Sleeper were officers of the Boston Theological Seminary and founded Boston University. Boston University's first offices and classrooms were in scattered locations in downtown Boston and on Beacon Hill, including the Old State House, the Old Corner Book Store, and Mount Vernon Place Congregational Church. In the 1930s, under Pres. Daniel L. Marsh, BU developed its central campus between Commonwealth Avenue and the Charles River near the Cottage Farm Bridge, since renamed the BU Bridge.

1898

Northeastern University was founded with the goal of "discovery of community educational needs and the meeting of these in distinctive and serviceable ways." The university's structure allows for alternating terms of study with terms of work at an outside job. This program adds a dimension to education while it enables many students to pay for an education that might otherwise be out of reach.

1902

Trusts left by wholesale clothier John Simmons led to the founding of Simmons College in the Fenway, near the Isabella Stewart Gardner Museum.

It is the first to stand in New England for a utilitarian education for girls, while aiming not to neglect any influence that may broaden the students' outlooks and deepen their lives.
—HENRY LEFAVOUR, FIRST PRESIDENT OF SIMMONS COLLEGE

1946

Rabbi Israel Goldstein led a group that purchased the Waltham, Massachusetts, campus of Middlesex University. With the help of physicist Albert Einstein and others, Goldstein established the Albert Einstein Educational Foundation with the purpose of creating a Jewish university in Waltham.

1948

Through contributions from the Jewish communities of Boston and elsewhere, Brandeis University was founded in Waltham,

Massachusetts. Like Boston College, the school welcomed students of all denominations. Abram Sachar served as first president of Brandeis. There were 107 students in the first freshman class.

1963

Architect Jose Luis Sert and associates helped Boston University construct four major buildings: the George Sherman Union, Mugar Memorial Library, Pappas Law Library, and the Law Tower. These buildings became the central focus of the university's long, narrow urban campus and shifted its orientation away from Commonwealth Avenue toward the Charles River. The papers of George Bernard Shaw, Theodore Roosevelt, H. G. Wells, Bette Davis, and Ella Fitzgerald are housed in the Mugar Library.

1969

Black students advocating a black studies program and minority scholarships at Brandeis seized Ford Hall and occupied the building for eleven days.

1998

In 1998, sixty-five colleges and universities could be found within a thirty-mile radius of Boston.

Massachusetts General Hospital and Other Medical Facilities

1810

Q: Who founded the Massachusetts General Hospital?
A: In August, two professors from the recently opened Harvard Medical School, Dr. John C. Warren and Dr. James Jackson, wrote a letter seeking to interest prominent people in the creation of a general hospital.

1812

The *New England Journal of Medicine,* the oldest continuously published medical journal in the world, was founded.

1816

The Massachusetts General Hospital, a.k.a. Mass General or MGH, received its charter from the state. The Massachusetts legislature provided granite, a site near the Charles River, and convict labor to assist in construction. MGH is the third oldest general, nonmilitary hospital in the country.

1846

The first operation using general anesthesia took place at MGH. Dr. Warren performed the operation to remove a tumor from the jaw of Gilbert Abbott after Dr. William Morton had administered ether. After the operation, the patient stated, "I have felt no pain."

1847

The first anesthesia administered in an American maternity ward was used at the Boston Lying-In Hospital.

1866

Doctors at MGH were the first to describe appendicitis and to recommend surgical treatment for it.

1929

The first iron lung was used to save the life of a polio patient at the Peter Bent Brigham Hospital.

1947

The Children's Cancer Research Foundation was established as one of the world's first centers for research and treatment of pediatric cancer.

1948

A twelve-year-old boy with cancer known as "Jimmy" made a radio appearance to help launch the Boston-based Jimmy Fund, which has since raised more than $150 million for cancer research.

1953

The Boston Red Sox made the Jimmy Fund their official charity.

1954

Doctors at what was then the Peter Bent Brigham Hospital performed the world's first successful kidney transplant.

1962

The first successful replantation of a severed human limb was performed at MGH.

1967

The first open-heart surgery was performed at Boston Children's Hospital.

1969

CCRF was expanded to treat cancer patients of all ages and renamed Dana-Farber Cancer Institute after Dr. Sidney Farber, whose research into chemotherapy led to the first complete remissions in children with leukemia, and for the Charles A. Dana Foundation. More than half of Dana-Farber's patients leave the institute cancer-free, and more than two-thirds of the children treated at the institute's Jimmy Fund Clinic are cured.

1980

Three of Boston's leading hospitals, the Peter Bent Brigham, the Robert B. Brigham, and the Boston Hospital for Women, merged to form the Brigham and Women's Hospital. Brigham and Women's is now one of the five major teaching hospitals of the Harvard Medical School.

1987

A research team at MGH led by Rudoph Tanzi identified a gene responsible for one form of Alzheimer's disease.

1993

MGH doctors were codiscoverers of the genes for Huntington's disease and Lou Gehrig's disease.

1995

Rudoph Tanzi's research team identified the second and third genes responsible for various forms of Alzheimer's disease.

1998

Carl Einar Gustafson, age sixty-two, emerged from anonymity to sign autographs at the Dana-Farber Cancer Institute. Gustafson revealed that he was the twelve-year-old "Jimmy" who made the radio appearance that helped to launch the Jimmy Fund in 1948. It was Dr. Sidney Farber who gave Gustafson the pseudonym "Jimmy" and who directed the treatment that cured Gustafson's illness.

The Museum of Fine Arts

1870

Needing more room to display their collections, the Boston Athenaeum, MIT, and Harvard persuaded the state legislature to charter the Boston Museum of Fine Arts. The museum's first building opened in Copley Square on July 3, 1876.

1877

Q: How did the museum's famous Asian collection get its start?
A: Zoologist Edward Sylvester Morse went to Japan to study brachiopods. Although he knew little about art, Morse became fascinated with things Japanese, especially pottery, which he began collecting. Morse contacted Charles Eliot Norton about a post at Tokyo's Imperial University and helped bring young philosopher and scholar of arts Ernest Fenollosa to Japan.

Morse returned and became director of what is now the Peabody Museum of Salem, and he became a more avid collector of Japanese art. A series of lectures he delivered at the Lowell Institute induced numerous rich or scholarly Bostonians to go to Japan, including Dr. William Sturgis Bigelow, Dr. Charles Goddard Weld, Percival Lowell, and Mr. and Mrs. John Lowell Gardner. With the help of these collectors and benefactors, Fenollosa, Okakura Kakuzo, and Kojiro Tomita, Boston's Museum of Fine Arts developed the finest collection of Asian art in the Western Hemisphere.

Otto Grundmann and other painters and teachers established the School of the Museum of Fine Arts.

1879

William Morris Hunt died. Hunt had persuaded Boston collectors to donate some seventy paintings and pastels by Jean François Millet, famed for his paintings of peasants, to the Museum of Fine Arts. Hunt, who favored an emotional and impressionistic direction in the arts, influenced Bostonian and American artistic taste.

1895

Edward Perry Warren and John Marshall began intense surveillance of the European auction market, concentrating on building a collection of classical art for the MFA. New York's Metropolitan Museum did not enter the field until at least a decade later.

1905

The Harvard University–Museum of Fine Arts Egyptian Expedition was established under the direction of Dr. George A. Reisner. In 1872 the museum had received mummies and other objects collected earlier by Robert Hay. In 1875 the museum received granite sculptures from the great temple at Karnak. These had been collected by John Lowell, who had given up the textile business when his wife died. He departed for Egypt and points east (he died in Bombay).

1907

Construction of MFA's current quarters between Huntington Avenue and the Fenway began. Construction followed an ambitious plan designed by Guy Lowell.

1917

Dr. Denman W. Ross gave his collection of the art of India to the MFA.

1934

G. H. Edgell became director of MFA. Edgell was the first MFA director to have a strong personal interest in European and American painting. This was the first year in which MFA welcomed more than half a million visitors.

1945

MFA's Asiatic, Painting, and Print Departments collaborated to mount an interdisciplinary temporary exhibition, "A Thousand Years of Landscape, East and West."

1948

The collection of John T. Spaulding was shown in a special MFA exhibition. One of Spaulding's lifelong goals as a collector had been to select paintings that would augment the museum's collection, and he often loaned the museum paintings during his lifetime. Not until his will was read did it become known that he had bequeathed his extensive collection of paintings to the MFA. Spaulding's collection included works by Cezanne, Manet, Degas, van Gogh, Winslow Homer, and Edward Hopper.

At the old Huntington Avenue entrance to the Boston Museum of Fine Arts, a Plains Indian appears moved by the museum's 1998 Monet exhibit.

1951

The M. and M. Karolik Collection of American Paintings, 233 canvases painted between 1815 and 1865, went on display at MFA.

1955

Perry Rathbone became the sixth director of MFA. Rathbone's first exhibition, "Sport in Art," included a fashion show and an ice-skating exhibition by Olympian Tenley Albright on a temporary rink installed in the museum.

1956

Director Perry Rathbone's first major exhibition was "Sargent's Boston," commemorating the centennial of the birth of painter John Singer Sargent.

1964

Aided by a four-day special exhibition in memory of Pres. John F. Kennedy, the museum attracted a new record of 830,007 visitors for the year. Some 139,000 of those attended the museum during the four days of the Kennedy display.

1995

Malcolm Rogers became director of MFA after serving as deputy director of London's National Portrait Gallery. Rogers's first moves were to cut the museum staff by 20 percent and to reopen the museum's inactive Huntington Avenue entrance.

The Isabella Stewart Gardner Museum

1899

A few weeks after her husband Jack's sudden death, Isabella Stewart Gardner bought land in Boston's Fenway to build a villa to house her art collection. Much of the building was imported from Italy, as well as other European sources.

Q: How did Isabella shock Boston society?
A: Isabella Stewart was a New Yorker transplanted to Boston when she married John Lowell Gardner and became known as "Mrs. Jack." She enjoyed shocking her social circle. She accomplished this by converting to Buddhism—and also by walking lion cubs on a leash down Tremont Street. Another of Isabella's shockers was John Singer Sargent's portrait of her in a black dress with a plunging neckline, emphasized by her pearls. Her usually tolerant husband insisted that the painting not be shown during his lifetime.

In 1886 the Gardners agreed to provide a scholarship for twenty-two-year-old Harvard fine arts scholar Bernard Berenson. Berenson proved to be a genius at finding masterpieces that could be acquired at bargain prices, and he helped Isabella purchase works by Botticelli, Raphael, Titian, Rembrandt, Vermeer, and others.

Isabella's collection grew to be one of the greatest private collections in the world.

The museum was not opened to the public until Isabella's death in 1925. It is a unique combination of extravagance, elegance, and tradition, of New York, Boston, and Europe. Visitors to the museum may experience an unusually deep peacefulness, or they may commune with the mischievous ghosts of art and history.

1990

On March 18, some $200 million worth of paintings and other objects were stolen from the Gardner Museum. Auction houses Christie's and Sotheby's offered a $1 million reward for return of the works.

The Arnold Arboretum

1806

Benjamin Bussey bought more than fifty acres of land in West Roxbury from Eleazar Weld, the seventh generation of Welds to live on the property. Governor Winthrop had given the property to Capt. Joseph Weld in 1640.

1846

A few generations ago, an almost unbroken forest covered the continent. The smoke from the Indian's wigwam rose only at distant intervals; and to one looking from Wachusett or Mt. Washington, the small patches laid open for the cultivation of maize interrupted not perceptibly the dark green of the woods. Now, those old woods are everywhere falling. The axe has made, and is making, wanton and terrible havoc. The cunning foresight of the Yankee seems to desert him when he takes the axe in hand. The new settler clears in a year more acres than he can cultivate in ten, and destroys at a single burning many a winter's fuel, which would be better kept in reserve for his grandchildren.

—GEORGE BARRELL EMERSON, *REPORT ON THE TREES AND SHRUBS GROWING NATURALLY IN MASSACHUSETTS*, 1846

The Public Garden Foot Bridge, designed by Clemens Herschel and William G. Preston, first felt footfalls in 1867.

1872

Using cash bequeathed by whaling merchant James Arnold and land left by Benjamin Bussey, the Arnold Arboretum was established. George Barrell Emerson, one of the trustees of Arnold's bequest, communicated his concept of an arboretum to Harvard College. Botanist Asa Gray, who had long been advocating an ambitious botanical garden, influenced Arnold and Emerson.

> *The Arnold Arboretum . . . shall contain . . . all the trees, shrubs, and herbaceous plants, either indigenous or exotic, which can be raised in the open air at said West Roxbury.*
> —GEORGE BARRELL EMERSON

1873

Charles Sprague Sargent became director of the Arnold Arboretum.

1882

A partnership with the city was finalized and more land acquired. Frederick Law Olmsted worked with Sargent on the arboretum's plan.

1895

The number of people who visit the Arboretum from curiosity, to enjoy its sylvan beauties, or to avail themselves of the opportunity to study its collections, appears to be increasing rapidly, and its educational value as a great object lesson must already be considerable.

—Charles Sprague Sargent

Walking stick in hand, Edward Everett Hale, author of "The Man Without a Country," helps a father watch the kids in Boston Common.

7

Transcendental Meditations

Literature and art from Bradstreet to Emerson to Winslow Homer to Updike to Robert B. Parker

> *Tomorrow night I appear for the first time before a Boston audience—*
> *4,000 critics.*
> —MARK TWAIN, LETTER TO PAMELA CLEMENS MOFFET, 1869

DESPITE THE PUBLISHING CONGLOMERATES and literary agents based in turn-of-the-millennium New York, despite London's esteemed Booker Prize for novelists, Boston continues, as it has since its earliest days, to lay claim to being the literary center of the English-speaking world.

Bostonian transcendentalism remains America's only native literary-philosophical movement, and it continues to influence many of the nation's novelists and poets more than most of them realize. The abolitionist and feminist movements, which had their American origins in Boston, also exercise enormous influence.

Harvard University is a center of American and English letters. Other universities, from the Ivy League to Iowa, have made and continue to make their contributions. But Harvard has spawned by far the most literary figures and attracted vast numbers of others as visitors.

Braggadocio aside, the literary spirit has undoubtedly flourished in Boston ever since the hermit William Blackstone brought his books and journals to Beacon Hill.

> I opened my eyes & let what would pass through them into the soul. I saw no more my relation how near and petty to Cambridge or Boston, I heeded no more what minute or hour our Massachusetts clocks might indicate—I saw only the noble earth on which I was born.
>
> —RALPH WALDO EMERSON, JOURNALS (1834)

1630

Q: Who was America's first poet?

A: Anne Bradstreet arrived in Boston with the Puritans on the ship *Arbella.* In 1631 she settled in a home in the center of what is now Harvard Square, Cambridge. She had eight children and wrote more than four hundred pages of verse.

1639

Cotton Mather's father, Increase Mather, was born in Boston, attended Harvard, and wrote 130 books.

1640

The *Bay Psalm Book,* the first book printed in the colonies, was published in Cambridge by Stephen Day.

1661

In Cambridge, minister John Eliot published the first edition of the Bible translated into an Indian language, Natick.

1662

Boston appointed the first official censor in the country. The post was not abolished until censor Richard Sinnot retired in 1975.

1663

Cotton Mather was born in Boston, attended Harvard, and wrote 444 books.

*His truer self was a power-crazed mind, bent on destroying
darkness with darkness, on applying his cruel, high-minded,
obsessed intellect to the extermination of witch and neurotic.*
                                                    —ROBERT LOWELL

Cotton and Increase Mather are buried in the Copps Hill Burying
Ground in Boston's North End.

1700

Q: Who published the country's first protest against slavery?
A: Samuel Sewall published America's first tract against slavery.

1750

Puritan Boston prohibited the performance of plays.

1755

Gilbert Stuart was born. The painter is renowned for his portraits
of George and Martha Washington. Less well known is the fact
that Stuart was the first to call Boston "the Athens of America."

1773

Poems on Various Subjects Religious and Moral by Phillis Wheatley
was published in England. Wheatley was brought to Boston from
Senegal as a slave. She learned English quickly and well. Her first
book was published when she was twenty years old. Freed in the
same year, Wheatley is said to have married unhappily and delivered three children who died in infancy. She herself died soon after,
at age thirty.

1794

Architect Charles Bulfinch built the city's first theater, which had
to advertise itself not as a theater but as "a school of virtue."

CA. 1800

Thomas Fleet, son-in-law of Elizabeth Vergoose, published her
"Mother Goose Songs." Mother Goose lived on what is now

Preacher Cotton Mather and his clan are among the colonists buried in Copp's Hill Burial Ground in Boston's North End.

Devonshire Street, but the dates of her birth and death and the whereabouts of her grave are unknown.

1803

Ralph Waldo Emerson was born and grew up in what is now downtown Boston. His family's cow grazed on Boston Common. In 1832 Emerson, having lost much of his conventional faith, "was dismissed at his own request" as a pastor and moved from Boston to the western suburb of Concord. Thereafter, Emerson frequently visited Boston on Saturdays, stopping at the Old Corner Book Store and dining at the Parker House, often with Henry Wadsworth Longfellow, John Greenleaf Whittier, James Russell Lowell, and Oliver Wendell Holmes, a group that took the name the "Saturday Club."

After 1857, some of the group began referring to themselves as the "Magazine Club." They began publishing a magazine called, after Holmes's suggestion, the *Atlantic Monthly.*

Mr. Emerson's English was as new to me as that of any of his con-
temporaries, but in his case I soon felt that the thought was as
novel as the language, and that both marked an epoch in literary
history. The grandiloquence . . . now appears to me to have been
the natural expression of an exhilaration of mind. . . . The intel-
lect of the time had outgrown the limits of Puritan belief.
—JULIA WARD HOWE, "FIRST YEARS IN BOSTON,"
REMINISCENCES, 1819–99

1804

Nathaniel Hawthorne was born in Salem on the Fourth of July.
From 1839 to 1841 Hawthorne worked as "weigher and gauger"at
the Boston Custom House. After that, the writer spent eight
months at the Brook Farm utopian community in West Roxbury.
One of Hawthorne's ancestors, John Hathorne, was a magistrate
who helped to send Sarah Good, Sarah Osborne, and the slave
Tituba to Boston for trial as witches.

1809

Oliver Wendell Holmes, poet, essayist, and professor of medicine
at Harvard, was born. Written when Holmes was twenty-one, his
poem "Old Ironsides" kept the USS *Constitution* from being
destroyed. He styled himself "autocrat of the breakfast table."
Today Holmes is often confused with his more famous son, Oliver
Wendell Holmes Jr., who served as a Supreme Court justice for
thirty years.

Also in this year, Edgar Allan Poe was born in a theatrical trunk in
Boston, to parents who were traveling actors.

Q: What did Poe think of Boston?
A: Commenting on the cliquishness of Boston writers, Poe later
called the city "Frogpondium."

1827

Poe's first book, *Tamerlane and Other Poems,* signed "by a Bostonian," was printed on Washington Street in Boston. Only about a

dozen copies of the first edition are known to exist—probably one or two remain to be found in New England attics. A newly discovered copy sold for $198,000 in 1988.

While he was in the army, Poe was stationed briefly at Fort Independence on Castle Island in Boston Harbor. There he heard a true story of revenge involving an officer being chained alive within the spaces of a stone wall. The event became the basis of more than one classic short story. In 1905 workmen found the actual Fort Independence skeleton.

1829

William Lloyd Garrison, age twenty-three, gave his first public speech against slavery on the Fourth of July. Two years later Garrison founded his magazine, the *Liberator*. Other noted Boston abolitionists included Angelina and Sarah Grimke, Lucretia Mott, Lydia Maria Child, and Lucy Stone, editor of the suffragist *Women's Journal*.

Today, a statue of Garrison stands on Commonwealth Avenue between Dartmouth and Exeter Streets. It bears an inscription from the first issue of the *Liberator*: "I am in earnest—I will not equivocate—I will not excuse—I will not retreat a single inch—and I will be heard." Commenting on the statue and on Garrison's mix of pacifism and passion, James Russell Lowell composed a couplet:

> There's Garrison, his features very
> benign for an incendiary.

1834

William Ticknor founded his publishing house, which became Ticknor and Fields in 1854. The firm published Hawthorne, Thoreau, Holmes, Longfellow, Lowell, and Emerson. It acquired the *Atlantic Monthly* in 1859, and James T. Fields became the magazine's editor. Today's Houghton Mifflin publishing company evolved from Ticknor and Fields.

1835

In Cambridge, the Mount Auburn Cemetery, America's first garden cemetery, was chartered. Writers buried here include:

Julia Ward Howe

Harriet A. Jacobs

Henry Wadsworth Longfellow

Amy Lowell

James Russell Lowell

Francis Parkman

V. R. Lang

Louis Agassiz

John Bartlett

Buckminster Fuller

Across the street in the Cambridge Public Cemetery are the graves of William Dean Howells, Henry James, William James, and Alice James.

Richard Henry Dana Jr. was forced to take a break from his junior year at Harvard due to eye problems. Dana signed on as a crewman on a California-bound ship and five years later at age twenty-five published *Two Years Before the Mast*. He went on to become a lawyer, writing a manual on maritime law and frequently donating his services to defend runaway slaves and those who helped them.

1836

The Transcendental Club began to meet at Emerson's house in Concord. Members included Margaret Fuller, author of *Woman in the Nineteenth Century*, and Elizabeth Palmer Peabody, editor, educator, bookseller, and publisher credited with opening America's first kindergarten.

> *Male and female represent the two sides of the great radical dualism. But, in fact, they are perpetually passing into one another. Fluid hardens to solid, solid rushes to fluid. There is no wholly masculine man, no purely feminine woman.*
> —MARGARET FULLER, WOMAN IN THE NINETEENTH CENTURY (1845)

Painter Winslow Homer was born in Boston.

1837

Henry Wadsworth Longfellow arrived in Cambridge as a professor of modern languages at Harvard and rented a room on Brattle Street in what would eventually become known as the Longfellow House. The house was already fabled for its many famous guests, including George and Martha Washington.

Longfellow's rhythmic narrative poems were immensely popular and successful. Many remain well known and entertaining today if not highly respected for innovation. Most famous are "The Midnight Ride of Paul Revere," "Hiawatha," "Evangeline," "The Courtship of Myles Standish," and "The Village Blacksmith."

When Longfellow married Frances Appleton in 1843, her wealthy father bought the house for the couple as a gift. It was an ill-fated gift, for eighteen years later Frances ("Fanny") died of burns suffered in the house when her dress caught fire as she applied hot wax to locks of her daughter's hair. Longfellow's face was scarred by burns suffered as he tried to rescue his wife.

1838

Poet and essayist Jones Very committed himself to McLean Psychiatric Hospital in Boston's Belmont suburb. A Harvard professor, Very wrote an essay on Shakespeare while at McLean that he said had been dictated to him by the Holy Ghost.

Numerous writers and artists have since spent time at McLean. Most well known are the poets Robert Lowell and Sylvia Plath and singer James Taylor. Many other excellent writers have sojourned there, including novelist Faye Levine and poet-activist Beatrice Hawley.

1841

George and Sophia Ripley founded Brook Farm as a utopian intellectual community on 170 acres in Boston's West Roxbury section.

We are a little wild here with numberless projects of social reform. Not a reading man but has a draft of a new Community in his waistcoat pocket.

—Ralph Waldo Emerson

1843

Boston historian William Hickling Prescott published his *History of the Conquest of Mexico,* followed four years later by *History of the Conquest of Peru.* Prescott's achievement is especially notable because an eye injury, sustained during an undergraduate food fight, had severely damaged his vision.

During the mid-nineteenth century, poet and literary historian William Corbett noted, "Boston abounded in historians who produced a body of work unparalleled for its scope and emphasis on story."

Boston's most prominent historian in this period was Francis Parkman, whose seven-volume *The Oregon Trail* narrated the French-English conflict. He also wrote about Champlain, LaSalle, and the Jesuits. Like Prescott, Parkman suffered from failing vision, and for much of his career is said to have been able to read for only a minute at a time.

Other noted historians of the period included George Bancroft, who between 1834 and 1876 published a ten-volume history of the United States, and John Lothrop Motley who published *The Rise of the Dutch Republic* in 1856.

Henry James was born in Cambridge. James would go on to write, in addition to his many novels and stories set in Europe

When a cannonball bounced off the USS Constitution *during the War of 1812, a sailor shouted, "Good God! Her sides are made of iron!"*

and elsewhere, numerous works set in Boston, perhaps most notably *The Bostonians.*

1844

Doubt not, O poet, but persist. Say "It is in me, and shall out." Stand there, balked and dumb, stuttering and stammering, hissed and hooted, stand and strive, until at last rage draw out of thee that dream-power which every night shows thee is thine own; a power transcending all limit and privacy, and by virtue of which a man is the conductor of the whole river of electricity.
—RALPH WALDO EMERSON, "THE POET"

1852

Q: How many copies of *Uncle Tom's Cabin* were sold in the book's first year?

A: Harriet Beecher Stowe's antislavery novel was published in Boston by John P. Jewett and sold 305,000 copies in its first year.

Harriet A. Jacobs, author of an autobiography entitled *Incidents in the Life of a Slave Girl,* was freed. Jacobs had faked her escape from slavery in North Carolina and hid for seven years while arranging for the escape of her two children. Ultimately she reached Boston's North End, where she worked as a dressmaker and later ran a boarding house in Cambridge. She is buried in Mount Auburn Cemetery.

1853

Ernest Fenollosa was born. Fenollosa was an Oriental studies scholar and a curator at the Boston Museum of Fine Arts. His notes on Chinese and Japanese language and literature were given to Ezra Pound after Fenollosa's death, and they became the basis of many of Pound's translations and adaptations and the foundation of his theories of poetry.

1854

Henry David Thoreau published *Walden,* celebrating independence, self-reliance, and love of nature.

*The fate of the country . . . does not depend on what kind of
paper you drop in the ballot-box once a year, but on what kind of
man you drop from your chamber into the street every morning.*
—HENRY DAVID THOREAU, *SLAVERY IN MASSACHUSETTS*, 1854

In May, Anthony Burns was tried for violating the Fugitive Slave
law. Lawyer Wendell Phillips and preacher Theodore Parker were
charged with inciting a riot when they spoke about the trial at
Faneuil Hall.

Thomas Wentworth Higginson, famous as Emily Dickinson's
only noted literary correspondent, led a failed attempt to free
Burns at the courthouse. Higginson, who later led black troops
during the Civil War, sustained a scar on his chin during the effort
and displayed it as a badge of honor thereafter. Higginson wrote
biographies of Longfellow and Whittier and was a secret supporter
of radical abolitionist John Brown. Higginson was born in Cambridge and spent much of his life there.

1855

John Bartlett, owner of the University Book Store in Cambridge
and renowned for identifying quotations, published a book titled
Familiar Quotations.

1862

Q: Who wrote a famous song and originated Mother's Day?
A: Julia Ward Howe, who married a Bostonian and became a
       Boston literary personality, wrote "The Battle Hymn of the
       Republic" in Washington, D.C., inspired by the sound of
       Union soldiers marching in the streets. Howe is also remem-
       bered as the founder of Mother's Day.

*I count it as one of my privileges to have listened to a single
sermon from Dr. Channing. . . . Its theme must have been
divine love; for Dr. Channing said that God loved black men
as well as white men, poor men as well as rich men, and bad
men as well as good men. The doctrine was quite new to me,
but I received it gladly.*
—JULIA WARD HOWE, *FIRST YEARS IN BOSTON, REMINISCENCES*, 1819–99

On a visit to Cambridge, western writer Bret Harte observed, "You cannot shoot in any direction without bringing down the author of one or two volumes."

Emily Dickinson of Amherst, Massachusetts, wrote to Thomas Wentworth Higginson, asking him, "Are you too deeply occupied to say if my verse is alive?" Higginson was intrigued but told Emily the poems were not strong enough to publish. He may have meant not that they were not good enough, but that the poems' delicacy and strangeness would have left them vulnerable to misunderstanding or critical attack. Higginson also called Emily's poems "remarkable, though odd."

Dickinson and Higginson continued to correspond, and after her death in 1886, he helped to arrange for Dickinson's work to be published. Higginson altered some of Emily's words and punctuation, but later editors have endeavored to restore the originals. Dickinson, who produced nine hundred poems and is arguably America's greatest poet, lived a reclusive life in western Massachusetts, but her mental life focused often on Boston, as well as points beyond.

1868

Louisa May Alcott published *Little Women*. Alcott grew up in Concord and moved to Boston's Louisburg Square toward the end of her life.

1871

Novelist William Dean Howells became editor of the *Atlantic*. Howells would later write a classic novel about a Boston industrialist, *The Rise of Silas Lapham*. As an editor, Howells published much of the early work of Henry James.

1878

Painter Ignaz Marcel Gaugengigl arrived in Boston from Bavaria. Gaugengigl painted numerous portraits of Bostonians as well as miniature historical scenes. He died in Boston in 1932.

Beacon Hill has become a posh place to live since hermit William Blackstone first settled there in 1625.

1883

Popular poet Kahlil Gibran, author of *The Prophet,* was born in Lebanon. A monument on Dartmouth Street facing the Boston Public Library commemorates the fact that Gibran grew up in Boston.

1885

Painter Frederick Childe Hassam painted *Rainy Day in Boston* and *Boston Common at Twilight.*

1887

Historian Samuel Eliot Morison was born in Boston. Specializing in naval history, Morison was the navy's official historian during World War II and later won the Pulitzer Prize for his biography of John Paul Jones.

1888

Boston's St. Botolph Club mounted the first solo exhibit of works by painter John Singer Sargent.

The first impression of many a well-bred Boston lady was that she had fallen into the brilliant but doubtful society one becomes familiar with in Paris or Rome. . . . [Sargent] actually presented people in attitudes and costumes that were never seen in serious, costly portraits before.
—GRETA, *ART IN BOSTON*, 1888

1896

The Boston Cooking School Cook Book was revised by Fannie Merritt Farmer. Farmer, limping from a childhood disease that may have been polio, enrolled in the school in 1888 at age thirty-one and five years later became its principal. When she finished her revision of the cook book, she brought it to a skeptical Houghton Mifflin Company, which only agreed to publish it at her expense. She taught careful measurement and scientific cookery with flair and imagination, and versions of her book have remained in print ever since.

Frederick William McMonnie's sculpture *Bacchante with Infant Faun* provoked controversy when architect Charles McKim tried to install it in the courtyard of the Boston Public Library. A Harvard professor called the nude figure "vile," and the Watch and Ward Society declared it "the glorification of that which is low and sensual and degrading." In 1897 library trustees asked McKim to withdraw the gift, and he sent it to New York's Metropolitan Museum of Art.

Maurice Prendergast, perhaps the most original of Boston's impressionist artists, painted *South Boston Pier.* Prendergast's work was not shown at the Museum of Fine Arts during his lifetime.

1902

Q: What was Amy Lowell's nickname?

A: Amy Lowell wrote her first poem on October 21 at the age of twenty-eight. Because she was born eighteen years after her brother, her family nicknamed her "Postscript." After reading about Ezra Pound's Imagist movement, Lowell traveled to London and became a leading Imagist.

1904

Art critic William Howe Downes counted some 600 professional painters, 350 architects, 100 engravers, 800 music teachers, and 12 theaters employing professional actors in Boston. The figures were presented in the essay "Boston as an Art Centre," written as a reply to Herbert Croly's 1903 article, "New York as an American Metropolis."

1927

Gordon Cairnie founded the Grolier Bookshop, an all-poetry store on Plympton Street near Harvard Square, with a friend. Cairnie ran the Grolier until his death in 1973. Since then the shop has been run by knowledgeable Harvard Square character and natural resource Louisa Solano.

1932

Poet Sylvia Plath was born in Winthrop and grew up in a house overlooking Boston Harbor. She moved to Wellesley, one of Boston's western suburbs, in 1942.

1937

John P. Marquand (not a Bostonian) won the Pulitzer Prize for his novel of a fictional Bostonian, *The Late George Appley.*

1943

Dazzling novelist Vladimir Nabokov took an apartment on Craigie Circle in Cambridge. Nabokov lectured on literature at Wellesley College and served as a research fellow specializing in butterflies at Harvard's Museum of Comparative Zoology.

1946

Poet Robert Lowell, a descendant of poets James Russell Lowell and Amy Lowell, won the Pulitzer Prize for his book *Lord Weary's Castle*.

1950

Novelist John Updike lived at Lowell House while he attended Harvard College. Updike is famed for his precise and glittering style, his wickedly accurate observation, his short stories, and many novels including *Rabbit Run, Roger's Version* (which relies heavily

Maritime historian Samuel Eliot Morison had not yet begun to fight when he won a Pulitzer Prize for his biography of John Paul Jones.

on Hawthorne's *The Scarlet Letter*) and his 1996 novel, which borrows its title from Julia Ward Howe, *In the Beauty of the Lilies.* Updike made another major contribution to Boston lore, his classic essay on the retirement of baseball immortal Ted Williams from the Boston Red Sox, "Hub Fans Bid Kid Adieu."

1953

Nobel Prize–winning dramatist Eugene O'Neill died in Boston and was buried under a pink quartz stone in the Forest Hills Cemetery, Jamaica Plain.

1956

Rhode Island native Edwin O'Connor published *The Last Hurrah,* a novel whose main character is a crooked Boston mayor whom O'Connor calls Frank Skeffington. Skeffington is based on former Boston mayor and convicted felon James Michael Curley.

Poet W. S. Merwin took an apartment on Beacon Hill. While living in Boston for twenty-one months, Merwin wrote his fourth book of poems, *The Drunk in the Furnace.*

1964

Malcolm X published his *Autobiography of Malcolm X,* ghost-written by Alex Haley. Malcolm grew up in Roxbury in the 1940s and converted to Islam at Boston's Norfolk Prison Colony. Both Malcolm and Ho Chi Minh worked as busboys at the Parker House.

> *Soon I ranged out of Roxbury and began to explore Boston proper. Historic buildings everywhere I turned, and plaques and markers and statues for famous events and men. One statue in Boston Common astonished me: a Negro named Crispus Attucks, who had been the first man to fall in the Boston Massacre. I had never known anything like it.*
> —*The Autobiography of Malcolm X*

1639–THE PRESENT

The roll call of writers who have passed through Harvard University as students lends the Boston-Cambridge area a unique literary cachet. Space does not permit a comprehensive list, but following is a sample:

Increase Mather	Van Wyck Brooks
Cotton Mather	e.e. cummings
Ralph Waldo Emerson	Gertrude Stein
Henry David Thoreau	T. S. Eliot
Oliver Wendell Holmes	Wallace Stevens
Richard Henry Dana Jr.	W. E. B. DuBois
Francis Parkman	Thomas Wolfe
Oliver Wendell Holmes Jr.	Charles Olson
William James	John Ashbery
Owen Wister	Adrienne Rich
Edward Arlington Robinson	William Burroughs
James Gould Cozzens	Norman Mailer
Countee Cullen	John Updike
George Santayana	Francine Prose
Robert Frost	Mark Helprin

1974

Pulitzer Prize–winning poet Anne Sexton committed suicide in the Boston suburb of Weston, where she was born in 1928.

1997

Mystery writers love Boston. Poe, who was born in Boston and signed his first book "by a Bostonian," though he didn't actually spend much time in the city, is often credited with inventing the detective story. The best-selling mystery writer of all time, Perry Mason's creator Erle Stanley Gardner, was born in Malden. More than 140 million copies of Gardner's books have been sold.

Boston's best-known detective today is probably Robert Parker's Spenser. The television series *Spenser for Hire* starring Robert Urich, assured Spenser's fame. Parker has written fourteen Spenser novels, beginning in 1973 with *The Godwulf Manuscript*.

Nancy Schon's 1987 bronze sculpture honors Robert McCloskey's book, Make Way for Ducklings.

> *Name's Spenser, with an S, like the poet. I'm in the Boston book. Under tough.*
>
> —ROBERT B. PARKER

Other eminent mystery writers whose PI's or victims often live or work in Boston include William G. Tapply, Linda Barnes, Jane Langton, and Sarah Smith. Barnes writes about detective Carlotta Carlyle and has also created Michael Spraggue. Langton's Homer Kelly is a former detective turned Harvard professor. So far Kelly has turned up in twelve novels, several bearing literary titles such as *Emily Dickinson Is Dead* and *The Transcendental Murders*. Soon after Langton published a book titled *Murder at the Gardner*, one of history's biggest art thefts took place at Boston's Gardner Museum. Langton earned a master's degree in art history at Harvard.

Built as a movie theater in 1925, the Wang Center for the Performing Arts now shelters music, dance, comedy, and tragedy.

8

Banned in Boston

Theater, movies, and television from The Orphan *to* Good Will Hunting

> *(Jefferson and his wife lock the door.)*
> JOHN ADAMS: *Good God, you don't mean they—they're not going to—in the middle of the afternoon?*
> BEN FRANKLIN: *Not everyone's from Boston, John.*
>
> —*1776* (1972)

LIKE THE HISTORIES OF other Boston institutions, the history of drama in Boston has been deeply marked by the conflict between Puritanism and the pleasure principle as well as by the downsizing of the city after its splendid early days. Theatrical performances have been repeatedly banned, and repeatedly they have returned to delight audiences and express the creativity of their principals.

Books and plays that have been banned in Boston include:

Strange Interlude, Eugene O'Neill
The Iceman Cometh, Eugene O'Neill
Who's Afraid of Virginia Woolf? Edward Albee
Lady Chatterley's Lover, D. H. Lawrence
Naked Lunch, William Burroughs

An American Tragedy, Theodore Dreiser
The Children's Hour, Lillian Hellman

The great Boston–New York rivalry has surfaced in drama, and on this stage New York seems, near the end of the twentieth century, to have won a decisive victory, if only because film and television have left room for only one center of living theater in the United States. Still, Boston has had its share of theatrical glories and memories. If it doesn't exactly flourish in Boston, drama is alive and well today in Boston's Charles Theater and the Boston Repertory Theater, among other homes.

Two of the more successful TV series of recent years have been set in Boston. *Cheers* and *Spenser for Hire* have portrayed the flavor of the city uncommonly well.

In the 1990s, Boston has pushed successfully to attract the filming of more major motion pictures in the city. Recent films that have been set or shot at least partially in Boston include:

Malcolm X (1992)
Celtic Pride (1996)
The Spanish Prisoner (1996)
Southie (1997)
Amistad (1997)
Good Will Hunting (1997)
A Civil Action (1998)
Next Stop Wonderland (1998)

Parts of *Amistad,* the story of a mutiny aboard a slave ship and the defense of freedom in America's courts, were filmed in the State House. *Good Will Hunting,* winner of two Oscars, is the story of a young man from South Boston whose brilliance enables him to succeed in the academic circles of Cambridge. The fact that films like these and a television show like *Cheers* have had recent success suggests that Boston's place in American history and the national psyche is being noticed in the 1990s.

1750

After an informal coffeehouse production of *The Orphan* by Thomas Ottway drew overflow crowds, the legislature banned all plays as "tending to increase immorality, impiety and a contempt of religion." The law was repealed in 1797.

1792

While performing plays was still against Massachusetts law, a group of British actors presented performances of *Othello* and *Romeo and Juliet,* calling them not plays but "moral lectures." The theater manager was arrested but released after a hearing, and the "moral lectures" continued. Patrons of the theater blamed Gov. John Hancock for the raid and trampled a picture of him.

1794

Q: Where was Boston's first theater?

A: Boston's first true theater, designed by Charles Bulfinch, was built on Federal Street at the corner of Franklin Street. Called the Boston Theater or the Federal Street Theater, the building burned down in 1798 and was immediately rebuilt.

1821

Noted English actor Edmund Kean scored major successes in February at the Federal Street Theater in *King Lear* and *Hamlet.* He then made the mistake of trying to do *Lear* and *Richard III* in May, when the weather was hot. Few people showed up, and Kean walked out without performing. He tried to return to Boston in 1825, having apologized in the press. But a crowd showed up to boo him off the stage, and he was forced to escape in disguise.

1843

The Baptist Society bought the Tremont Theater and converted it to a church. It was said that the society's motive was not merely to acquire a church building but to put a theater out of business. In the same year, the Boston Museum, built two years earlier to display paintings and stuffed animals, began to be used for plays, which proved highly successful.

> *[The Boston Museum was] a meeting place where those who did not wish to be regarded as theatregoers could visit without a blush. Many of the regular habitués of the Boston Museum, even after it had become much more of a theater, fondly believed they were not attending a regular playhouse.*
> —KATE RYAN, 1915

1845

Q: What was the "Old Howard"?

A: In 1845 Sheridan's *School for Scandal* was presented at the newly named Old Howard Athenaeum. Later known affectionately as the "Old Howard," the theater became the home of vaudeville, burlesque, and striptease shows in the 1920s. Historian Walter Muir Whitehill wrote that the Old Howard was "beloved by generations of bums, sailors, and Harvard undergraduates." Frequent patron Oliver Wendell Holmes was quoted in the *Saturday Evening Post* as commenting after an enjoyable show, "Thank God I am a man of low taste!"

Vaudeville and burlesque stars, celebrities, and future stars who appeared at the Old Howard included:

Fred Allen	The Marx Brothers
Bert Lahr	Fanny Brice
John L. Sullivan	Sophie Tucker
Jack Dempsey	Hindu Sam
Phil Silvers	Cassie French
Abbott and Costello	Ann Corio

1852

The Music Hall, now known as the Orpheum Theater, opened on Hamilton Place. The Boston Symphony Orchestra played its debut concert at the Orpheum in 1881. Booker T. Washington and Ralph Waldo Emerson lectured at the Orpheum.

1854

On Washington Street a new Boston Theater was opened.

Even today no theater in the world has been able to surpass it in all important particulars. In beauty of line, in acoustical properties, in ventilation, in ease and economy of heating, in generosity of entrances and lobbies, in comfort and celerity of exit, in size and capability of stage, it has been a model for all the large theaters in this country.

—Eugene Tompkins, 1908

1865

Q: What were the Booth brothers doing on April 14?

A: Edwin Booth, one of the greatest of American actors, was onstage at the Boston Theater on Washington Street on April 14 when his younger brother, John Wilkes Booth, shot Pres. Abraham Lincoln at Ford's Theater in Washington, jumped onto the stage, and escaped on horseback.

1876

Members of the Baptist, Methodist, and Episcopal churches founded the Watch and Ward Society in an attempt to keep watch on public morals. The Watch and Ward prevented some books from being sold and prompted the arrest of some who performed at the Old Howard.

1878

The first production in America of Gilbert and Sullivan's comic operetta *HMS Pinafore* took place on November 25 at the Boston Museum.

1889

The second Tremont Theater opened on Tremont Street near the Haymarket. In 1915 D. W. Griffith's pioneering movie *The Birth of a Nation* was show there, and the theater became a movie theater, the Astor, in 1949.

1891

A group of Bostonians put on *Margaret Fleming* by James A. Herne at Chickering Hall. With the realistic play dealing with contemporary illness and adultery, they hoped to create an American *theatre libre* following the example of the *Theatre Libre* that had opened in Paris four years earlier. The movement to create radical, contemporary drama spawned the Moscow Art Theater (1896) and the Irish Literary Theater (1899), renamed the Abbey Theater in 1904 and renowned, among other reasons, for the participation of poet William Butler Yeats. The Bostonian producers of *Margaret Fleming* were not successful in founding a company.

Q: Who originated the system of trying out plays in Boston before taking them to New York?

A: On February 9, 1891, Bostonian Charles H. Hoyt, a former *Boston Post* reporter, opened his comedy *A Trip to Chinatown* at the Boston Theater. After two weeks in Boston and some further tinkering in other cities, the play lasted for 657 New York performances. Hoyt was one of the first to develop the system of trying plays out in Boston before taking them to New York. His style of comedy was a forerunner of the works of George S. Kaufman, Moss Hart, and Neil Simon.

1894

B. F. Keith opened his B. F. Keith's Theater on Washington Street and began presenting variety shows that became known as vaudeville. Keith's has been called the birthplace of American vaudeville.

1900

On December 20, the Colonial Theater on Boylston Street opened with an elaborate production of *Ben Hur*. A dozen horses were brought onstage for the play's climactic chariot race. The sumptuous theater, decorated with murals and relief sculpture, seated seventeen hundred and was designed by architect Clarence H. Blackall. Thomas Edison helped to develop the theater's fine acoustics.

1904

Mayor Patrick Collins appointed John M. Casey to head the city's office that licensed theaters. Casey served for twenty-eight years as a guardian of theatrical morals, persuading companies to change their scripts or costumes or to stay away from Boston completely.

In the same year, Harvard professor George Pierce Baker, Boston Symphony founder Henry Lee Higginson, and Winthrop Ames joined in an attempt to turn the Castle Square Theater into a major Boston institution.

1906

Back from a study of European theaters, Winthrop Ames acquired a Boston site to build on then changed his mind and moved to New York to found his company there.

The 350-seat Theatre Comique, around the corner from the Old Howard, became the first Boston theater built specifically for films.

1908

One of the earliest silent films was *The Boston Tea Party* with Charles Ogle. Movies that have been set significantly or entirely in Boston or have been filmed at least partially in Boston include:

The Boston Tea Party (1908)
The Battle of Bunker Hill (1911)
The Return of Boston Blackie (1927)
Two Sisters from Boston (1946)
Mystery Street (1950)
The Last Hurrah (1958)
The Thomas Crown Affair (1968)
1776 (1972)
The Friends of Eddie Coyle (1973)
The Bostonians (1984)
Glory (1989)

1910

Boston's Shubert Theater opened on January 24 with a performance of Shakespeare's *Taming of the Shrew.*

1911

Q: How did William Butler Yeats influence Boston theater?
A: William Butler Yeats, Nobel prize poet and one of the founders of the Abbey Theater, lectured at Harvard. Yeats inspired a group of Bostonians including poet Amy Lowell to organize America's first little theater. The Toy Theater opened January 1, 1912, on Lime Street.

1914

The Wilbur Theater opened.

In the same year, Alexander Woollcott became theater critic for the *New York Times* and was banned from theaters owned by the Shubert brothers after an unfavorable review. The *Times* stood behind its critic, ending coverage of plays at Shubert theaters and refusing their advertising. Critics in New York and elsewhere began to write more honestly and boldly. The power of New York critics increased, which ultimately lent greater importance to tryouts in Boston of New York–bound shows.

1915

Boston had fifteen playhouses, four of them with their own resident companies. The situation was to change by 1932 when the last of the resident stock companies closed, leaving Boston theaters to serve primarily as places where shows on their way to New York could be tried out.

Australian actor Henry Jewett took over the Toy Theater, intending to give Boston a world-class company.

Blacks held protest marches in an attempt to stop the showing of D. W. Griffith's film *Birth of a Nation.* Boston representative William Sullivan filed a bill to ban the film, but efforts to stop the showing were unsuccessful.

1919

The founding of the Actors' Equity Association gave further impetus to the use of Boston as a tryout and preparation for presenting plays in New York. The union won for actors a small wage for the first four weeks of rehearsal, then full pay. Many plays needed much more than four weeks to be fine-tuned and ready, and companies had to start taking in money when actors went on full pay. So the need for tryout performances in Boston and other cities was substantial.

A passing Bostonian ignores one of the Common's less puritanical sculptures.

The Theater Guild of New York began that year, developing a subscription list of theatergoers first in New York, subsequently in Boston and other cities. The Boston subscription list reached a high-water mark of twenty thousand, but it had shrunk to less than half that number by the time the plan was dropped in 1977.

1925

As part of the continuing movement to give Boston a major theater, Henry Jewett opened the Repertory Theater of Boston on Huntington Avenue with a production of Sheridan's *The Rivals*. But Jewett died in 1928, leaving the theater in poor financial condition, perhaps due to competition from the movies, and two years later it closed.

The Irish make good Puritans.
—FRANK CHASE, HEAD OF THE WATCH AND WARD SOCIETY

1926

Boston's first commercial movie showing took place at the Colonial Theater. The moving picture was *Don Juan* starring Lionel Barrymore and featuring "Vitaphone accompaniment."

1929

Mayor Malcolm E. Nichols refused to allow Eugene O'Neill's play *Strange Interlude* to be performed in Boston, refusing all appeals and refusing to comment. The play went on at a movie theater in Quincy, just a few miles south of Boston.

> *Neither the mayor nor the Boston clergymen supporting him are in the least competent to censor plays.*
> —THE REVEREND RAYMOND A. CHAPMAN, VICAR OF
> ST. STEPHEN'S EPISCOPAL CHURCH

1932

Five years after the movie *The Jazz Singer* starring Al Jolson (and sound), there were an estimated 400 live theaters left in the entire country, down from some 4,000 in 1900. Of the survivors, 75 were in New York, 7 in Boston.

1933

The Watch and Ward Society succeeded in shutting down the Old Howard for thirty days.

> *I was continually badgered by the eager, lip-pursing members of the New England Watch and Ward society, who combined the fervor of bird-feeders and disciples of the Anti-Vivisection Society. For some time a group of shocked ladies had been urging me to close the Howard Athenaeum, better known as "The Old Howard."*
> *"I would like to honor your petition," I told the ladies, "but do you realize the historical significance of the Howard Athenaeum? You may think the Howard is well known, but the Old Howard is known in every port of the world. It is one of Boston's great institutions."*
> —JAMES MICHAEL CURLEY, *I'D DO IT AGAIN*, 1957

1935

On January 15, Mayor Frederick W. Mansfield banned Sean O'Casey's play *Within the Gates*. Two Jesuit priests, supported by a

Methodist minister, had written to the mayor that the play was
"drenched with sex and written to point out the futility of religion."
The Federal Theater of the Works Progress Administration began
producing plays at the former Repertory Theater.

With a few exceptions, those who acted here [in the Federal The-
ater] were second- or third-raters. However, they were the
Boston representatives of a project that was heroic in concept,
and that . . . might well have developed into a national theater.
. . . In New York, unfortunately, some of the most gifted theater
people of America . . . put on productions that attracted the ire
of some of the most obtuse members of Congress, and the entire
project, including of course the Boston company, was liquidated.
—ELLIOT NORTON, *BROADWAY DOWN EAST*

Porgy and Bess had its world premier at the Colonial Theater.

1938

Edwin Burr Pettet ran the New England Repertory Theater at various locations on Beacon Hill until 1945. Pettet later became chairman of the theater arts department at Brandeis University.

Thornton Wilder opened his play *The Merchant of Yonkers* at the
Colonial. He rewrote the unsuccessful script at a table in the Colo-
nial's lounge. The play later opened again at the Colonial as *The*
Matchmaker, with Ruth Gordon. The comedy still was not a great
success and would not become one until it opened later, in New
York, with music added, and was renamed *Hello, Dolly!*

1940

Battle of Angels, Tennessee Williams's first play to be produced,
opened and closed at Boston's Wilbur Theater. Its scheduled New
York run was aborted.

1943

Rodgers and Hammerstein opened their musical *Away We Go!* at
the Colonial Theater. In Boston they made some revisions and
considered changing the show's title to *Oklahoma!*

1947

Harvard student Jerome Kilty founded the Veterans' Theater Workshop. A year later he was able to convert the group into a professional troupe, the Brattle Theater Company. The company lasted until 1952.

1951

The *Boston Blackie* television series was set in Boston.

1953

Nobel laureate Eugene O'Neill died in Boston and was buried in the Forest Hills Cemetery, Jamaica Plain, under a pink quartz boulder.

1957

A company of Boston University students opened the Charles Playhouse with Sartre's *No Exit.* The company lasted until 1971. Since then the Charles has served as a venue for off-Broadway theater. Originally a church designed by Asher Benjamin, the building later housed the Lido Venice nightclub before becoming the theater that has survived into the 1990s.

1959

Harvard's Loeb Drama Center was designed by Hugh Stubbins.

1961

The American Civil Liberties Union contested attempts by Boston censors to force changes in the script of Edward Albee's *Who's Afraid of Virginia Woolf?* Subsequent presentation of the play in a preview version in New York, a less expensive tryout method than playing Boston, diminished the number of plays that would visit Boston for tryouts.

After a fire in 1961, the Old Howard was demolished, mourned by many but not by all.

1962

In the name of urban renewal, Scollay Square, a world-famous theater, burlesque, and pleasure district, was demolished.

1970

Richard J. Sinnott, Boston's last theater licensor, unofficially known as the city's censor, stopped the production of *Hair* for four weeks in March and April, not on account of the play's nudity but for what he saw as desecration of the American flag.

What I did take action against was the almost continuous desecration of the flag of the United States, and I almost died fighting for that flag and I think I have the right to speak up to protect the flag of the country I love. And I did this through the office of the district attorney, and the practice was ended immediately.

—RICHARD J. SINNOTT

1971

The Kennedy Center in Washington, D.C., opened and began attracting tryout runs that would previously have played Boston.

1975

The Red Devil Battery Sign by Tennessee Williams opened and closed at Boston's Shubert Theater. Its scheduled New York run was aborted.

1979

The short-lived television sitcom *Park Street Under* provided inspiration for the later Boston-based giant sitcom hit *Cheers*.

1982

Cheers debuted.

1993

Q: How long did *Cheers* run?

A: Inspired by Boston's Bull and Finch Pub, *Cheers* ran for eleven years, ending in 1993 when the 275th and final episode of the popular television sitcom was aired.

Q: Who were some famous Bostonians who made cameo appearances on *Cheers?*

A: Famous politicians who made guest appearances on the show included House Speaker Thomas "Tip" O'Neill, Boston Mayor Ray Flynn, and Gov. (and unsuccessful Democratic presidential nominee) Michael Dukakis. Boston athletes who appeared on the show included Red Sox pitcher Luis Tiant, Red Sox third baseman Wade Boggs, and Celtics forward Kevin McHale.

Major television shows that have been set in Boston include:

Boston Blackie (series, 1951)
Cheers (series, 1982)
Spenser for Hire (series, 1985)
Goodnight, Sweet Wife: A Murder in Boston (movie, 1990)
Original Sins (movie, 1995)
Boston Common (series, 1996)

1997

Q: What is the longest-running nonmusical play in United States history?

A: Marilyn Abrams and Bruce Jordan are the producers of *Shear Madness,* the longest-running nonmusical play in the history of the United States. An interactive comedy-mystery, *Shear Madness* by Swiss playwright Paul Portner was originally titled *Scherenschnitt.* In addition to Boston, the play was running in five other U.S. cities as well as Mexico City, Budapest, and Tel Aviv. The sixteen-year-old Boston company, the thirteen-year-old Chicago company, and the nine-year-old Washington company are listed in *The Guinness Book of World Records.* Boston's Warrenton Street, site of the Charles Playhouse, is officially known as "Shear Madness Alley."

The largely Irish enclave of South Boston, aka "Southie," was celebrated in the 1997 movie Good Will Hunting.

Boston comedians Jay Leno and Conan O'Brien currently dominate U.S. late-night television ratings. Bostonian Steven Wright is one of the country's leading stand-up comedians. Wright performed at the Orpheum in 1996.

Young Boston writer-actors Matt Damon and Ben Affleck received the Oscar for best screenplay for *Good Will Hunting,* filmed in South Boston and Cambridge. Damon, Affleck, and Robin Williams starred in the movie. Williams was awarded the 1998 Oscar for best supporting actor.

The Boston Globe, *shown here in its 1999 digs, opened less ritzy doors in 1872.*

9

Publick Occurrences

Boston's media: newspapers, radio, and television

The readers of the Boston Evening Transcript
Sway in the wind like a field of ripe corn.

—T. S. ELIOT

NEWSPAPERS, AS MIGHT BE expected, have flourished in Boston. Competition and creativity among journalists have been lively, and the newspapers have played an active role in historical events since the American Revolution.

Most unusual, perhaps, was William Lloyd Garrison's abolitionist newspaper, *Liberator*. This journal played a major role in Boston and in the national movement to end slavery.

Boston newspapers have affected elections with straightforward endorsements and arguments as well as with devious tricks, such as the *Boston Post* used to help defeat James Michael Curley in 1937. On election day the *Post* ran a box that read: "Voters of Boston! Cardinal O'Connell, in speaking to the Catholic Alumni Association, said, 'The walls are raised against honest men in civic life.' You can break down those walls by voting for an honest, clean, competent young man, Maurice J. Tobin." The cardinal had not actually endorsed Tobin, but the story made it sound as if he had.

The *Boston Globe* was the first newspaper in the country to call for Richard Nixon's resignation, and it was one of the first to publish the Pentagon Papers, documents that may have been influential in ending the Vietnam War.

Boston's newspapers have engaged in hijinks involving elephants, cats, and a variety of bizarre contests and stunts. The *Boston Post*, for example, once garnered publicity by asking children to contribute pennies and nickels to bring three elephants to Franklin Park Zoo. When the elephants were acquired and displayed at Fenway Park, some seventy thousand people showed up, twice as many as could fit in Fenway.

In the search for circulation, Boston papers have pioneered the concept of community involvement. Debates may rage over problems of objectivity and bias in the press and electronic media, but there is no denying that the media have played a role in the life of the community. Nearly everyone reads a newspaper and watches some news on television. The media have become part of the Bostonians' environment. Some significant stages of their evolution have taken place in Boston.

1690

Q: What was America's first newspaper, and how long was it published?

A: On September 25, Benjamin Harris printed America's first newspaper, *Publick Occurrences: Both Foreign and Domestic.* Because Harris commented on the brutality of British rule, this publication was immediately suppressed, never to appear again.

1704

Boston postmaster John Campbell, known as the father of modern journalism, started his *Boston News Letter.* Although much of its news consisted of clippings from months-old English newspapers that had just arrived by ship, the *Boston News Letter* survived for eleven years.

1719

A new paper, the *Gazette,* appeared. A critical comment published in the *Boston News Letter* may have inadvertently implied that there was a superior liveliness to the new entry: "I pity the readers of the new paper. Its sheets smell more strongly of beer than of midnight oil."

1793

Henry Ingraham Blake, called the father of American reporting, started the *Massachusetts Mercury.*

1830

The *Boston Transcript* was founded by Lynde Minshull Walter, Henry W. Dutton, and James Wentworth. The *Transcript* printed the U.S. Constitution in full every Wednesday.

1831

William Lloyd Garrison initiated the influential abolitionist journal *Liberator,* and in the same year the *Boston Post* began publishing. The *Post* was destined to become, for a time, the highest-circulation standard-size newspaper in the country.

1836

John Lowell, son of Francis Cabot Lowell, established the Lowell Institute, an educational institution that sponsored lectures and lecture series and that eventually evolved into Boston's pioneering public television station, WGBH.

1840

During the decade from 1830 to 1840, Boston, with a population of some ninety-three thousand, saw fifteen newspapers come and go, with as many as twelve coexisting at once.

1842

Q: Who was the first woman to edit a major American newspaper?

A: Cornelia Wells Walter began a five-year stint as editor of the *Boston Transcript.* She was the first woman in America to edit a major metropolitan newspaper. Talented and conservative, Walter opposed women's suffrage, criticized the evolutionary theories of botanist Asa Gray, and jousted with Edgar Allan Poe.

1848

Reporter and expert stenographer Stephen N. Stockwell caused a sensation by publishing verbatim a speech given by Daniel Webster in support of Zachary Taylor's presidential campaign.

1872

The *Boston Globe* began its life with the following announcement:

New daily paper in Boston. Will be published Monday, March 4, a new and independent morning commercial and business journal of the first class, and of the largest newspaper size. Its model and arrangement will be original, and the purpose will be to produce a journal equal in enterprise, ability, and intrinsic value, to any newspaper issued at home or abroad. Its editorial corps will embrace the ablest writers of the times, and its various departments will be in charge of competent and experienced persons. The newspaper will be known as The Boston Daily Globe, *and will commence with every mechanical appliance complete, including the most perfect and rapid steam presses, and with all the necessary means in its business department for securing accuracy and dispatch. In the interest of neither sect nor party, nothing will interfere with its plain and outspoken independence, while its endeavor will be, by consistency and fairness, to challenge the respect of an intelligent public. Terms—$12 per annum. Single copies four cents.*

Within two decades after the opening of the *Globe* at 92 Washington Street, the street between Milk Street and State Street began to be called the Fleet Street of Boston, or Newspaper Row. It was a short walk from newspaper row to either Boston City Hall or the State House.

The *Globe* was started by six businessmen, led by Jordan Marsh Company founder Eben Jordan, with an investment of $150,000. Within a year the *Globe* hired Gen. Charles H. Taylor as business manager.

1875

With advertisements from Jordan's Department Store and Mason and Hamlin Organ Company, the *Boston Globe* became the first newspaper in the country to run full-page ads.

1877

The first newspaper story ever filed by telephone was a *Boston Globe* report from Salem on a lecture by Alexander Graham Bell.

1878

The *Boston Herald* opened its publishing plant on Washington Street.

1882

Thompson's Spa opened on Newspaper Row and quickly became a center of city, state, and newspaper gossip. After hours the spa sold leftovers to impoverished reporters at cut rates.

Six years younger than the Globe, *the tabloid* Boston Herald *is a vigorous and energetic competitor.*

1883

The *Daily Advertiser* opened its Washington Street plant.

1886

Q: Where did bylines originate?

A: The *Globe's* circulation passed the one-hundred-thousand mark, making it the largest non–New York City newspaper outside in circulation. The *Globe* became the first newspaper to put reporters' bylines on their stories.

1891

Edward A. Grozier bought the *Boston Post.* The paper had three thousand paid subscribers and street circulation of about twenty thousand. Grozier had learned most of what he knew about newspapers working for Joseph Pulitzer in New York.

Boston had nine daily newspapers, four semiweeklies, and five biweeklies. Among the papers on newspaper row at this time were:

The Boston Journal	*The Boston Evening Record*
The Boston Post	*The Boston Courier*
The Boston Herald	*The Sunday Budget*
The Boston Advertiser	*The Saturday Evening Gazette*
The Boston Transcript	

1892

Perhaps to help it compete with the resurgent *Post,* the *Globe* offered a prize of $5 a week for life for the best estimate of the vote in the 1892 presidential race. The winner collected some $14,500 from the *Globe* before he died.

Q: How was the *Globe* embarrassed during the Lizzie Borden case?

A: The *Globe* suffered a serious setback in the same year. *Globe* reporter Henry G. Trickey was fed a false story by a private detective alleging that Lizzie Borden killed her father and stepmother because they had discovered she was pregnant. The story made front-page headlines, went on for page after page, and became the talk of the town. The *Herald* uncovered the hoax, and the *Globe* was forced to apologize.

1895

Following the death of Eben Jordan, General Taylor became half-owner of the *Globe*.

1897

The *Globe* printed its first color Sunday comics section.

1900

Pauline Hopkins edited the *Colored American*.

1901

About one hundred miles from Boston, Guglielmo Marconi, inventor of radio, built the first major radio transmitter to operate in America. Two years later, Pres. Theodore Roosevelt used it to send a greeting to England's Edward VII.

Humorist Cyrus Newkirk (byline—Newton Newkirk) began his daily "All Sorts" column for the *Boston Post*.

1902

Frank Munsey, owner of the *Washington Times* and the *New York Daily News,* bought the *Boston Journal* from Stephen O'Meara.

1904

William Randolph Hearst founded the *Boston American*. In 1917 he bought the *Advertiser* and in 1920 the *Record,* giving him morning, evening, and Sunday papers in Boston.

1905

Q: What sensational murder case helped build the *Post*'s circulation?
A: The *Post* built its circulation with days of sensational coverage of the dismemberment murder of Susan Geary of Cambridge

The New York Times *acquired the* Boston Globe, *truck and all, for $1.1 billion in 1993.*

after a botched abortion. The victim's remains, minus her head, were found in two separate suitcases floating in Boston Harbor. After the *Post* had published several false leads, leading to interrogations and arrests of innocent people, the newspaper scored a coup by hiring its own diver, who succeeded in finding the missing head.

1906

One of Edwin Grozier's most successful promotions was the creation of the *Post* Santa. The paper created a fund to provide toys for children of needy families. The *Post* would publish stories of the needy throughout the Christmas season and solicit donations. The *Boston Globe* bought the name and idea when the *Post* went out of business in 1956, and the *Globe* Santa continues today.

On Christmas Eve America's first radio program was broadcast from Marshfield, Massachusetts.

1908

Mary Baker Eddy started the *Christian Science Monitor* to cover not a single locality but "the daily activities of the entire world." Eddy forbade reporting of crimes or scandals. By 1919, circulation of the *Monitor* had passed 120,000.

1909

Post publisher Edwin Grozier acquired 431 ebony canes and began a promotion that involved giving a cane to the oldest resident of each town in which the paper was sold. The canes were inscribed and, on the death of the holder, were to be passed on to the new "oldest" resident. The *Post* would publish stories and photographs of the ceremonies. Many of the canes survived, and some continued to be passed on, even after the *Post* stopped publishing in 1956.

Grozier also ran numerous competitions—essay contests, sports predictions, puzzles, and the like.

1911

William Stanley Braithwaite was the *Transcript*'s literary editor, the first African American in the country to hold such a position on a major metropolitan newspaper.

The *Globe* hired Laurence L. Winship as a reporter.

1913

Q: Who was Joe Knowles?

A: One of the *Post*'s wildest promotional gimmicks was suggested by illustrator Joe Knowles, who volunteered to enter the Maine woods with nothing—not even clothing—and stay for sixty days. His only contact with humanity was to be dropping off stories and drawings done on birch bark with charcoal at an appointed spot in the woods. At first the stunt attracted little attention. For clothing and food, Knowles managed to kill a bear, some deer, and various birds.

Debate raged over whether Knowles was telling the truth. When he returned to Boston, a crowd variously estimated at between 150,000 and 400,000 jammed Washington Street to see the artist dressed in animal skins.

1914

In another *Post* promotion, Edwin Grozier asked Boston children to contribute pennies and nickels to bring three elephants, Molly, Waddy, and Tony, to the Franklin Park Zoo. When the elephants were introduced at Fenway Park, an overflow crowd of more than seventy thousand showed up.

1920

In July the *Post* published its first story on the schemes of Charles Ponzi, who was taking money from investors with the claim that he would invest it in international postal reply coupons and pay them 50 percent interest in forty-five days. Actually he was paying old investors with money taken from new ones. By July, he had taken in more than $6.4 million. The first *Post* story was not critical and led to more customers for Ponzi.

The *Post* then interviewed financial publisher Clarence W. Barron, who raised the question of why Ponzi was putting millions into bank accounts that paid 5 percent annually. When Ponzi closed his operation due to investigations by district attorneys and postal authorities, the *Post* reported that he was unlikely to reopen, causing a run of investors seeking their money back. Ponzi threatened to sue, but the *Post* did not back down.

Ponzi had hired publicist William McMasters as what has come to be called a "spin doctor." But in August, McMasters sold his story to the *Post,* asserting that Ponzi was insolvent and was not investing his customers' money in postal coupons. Ponzi threatened to sue Barron, McMasters, and the *Post.*

Post reporters discovered that Ponzi had spent time in jail for forgery in Montreal and printed the story in spite of Ponzi's threats. Two days later, Ponzi was arrested. The *Post* won a Pulitzer Prize for its reporting of Ponzi's schemes.

1921

Gen. Charles H. Taylor died, and his son William O. Taylor became principal owner of the *Globe*.

WBZ radio, the country's second commercial station, went on the air in Springfield, Massachusetts. The station moved to Boston three years later.

1923

Hindy, the *Post* cat, died. Hindy got his name when he wandered into the *Post* building and killed another cat in a fight. Reporters called the new alley cat von Hindenberg, eventually shortened to Hindy. Pulitzer Prize–winning reporter Herb Baldwin started writing humorous stories from the cat's point of view, signed with Hindy's byline. When one reader wrote asking for a picture of Hindy, Baldwin wrote a story in the cat's voice offering pictures on request. The managing editor argued against running the story because it was too ridiculous; nobody would want a picture of an

The city's two daily newspapers, the Boston Globe *and the* Boston Herald, *sell quickly on Commonwealth Avenue.*

alley cat. City editor Edward J. Dunn speculated that 5,000 people would ask for a picture. The story ran, and the *Post* filled 112,000 requests for Hindy's picture.

1930

One of the *Post*'s biggest scoops ever was the surrender of Prohibition-era policeman and liquor czar Oliver B. Garrett. Garrett had made a fortune in graft from Boston-area speakeasies. One of the tricks that kept his operations going was to raid clubs that were paying him off and have their liquor poured down the sink—the clubs were equipped with special sinks that caught and saved the valuable stuff.

Finally, Garrett was demoted to street duty and filed a pension claim. During investigation of the claim, many of his other activities were uncovered. He disappeared and for five months became the focus of a nationwide manhunt. When Garrett decided to surrender he wrote to *Boston Post* crime reporter Lawrence R. Goldberg and gave him a detailed, exclusive story.

1937

Q: How did the *Post* help defeat James Michael Curley?

A: Through a tricky stratagem, the *Post* helped defeat James Michael Curley in his race for mayor against Maurice Tobin. It was a close election, and on election day the *Post* ran a front-page box that read: "Voters of Boston! Cardinal O'Connell, in speaking to the Catholic Alumni Association, said, 'The walls are raised against honest men in civic life.' You can break down those walls by voting for an honest, clean, competent young man, Maurice J. Tobin."

Not noticing the final quotation marks, most readers thought, as they were almost certainly intended to, that the cardinal had endorsed Tobin, when in fact he had done no such thing. Curley frantically tried to find the cardinal to secure a fast retraction or clarification, but the cardinal could not be reached on election day. Curley lost by twenty-five thousand votes.

1941

The *Boston Transcript,* which had regularly published genealogies of Boston's leading families, closed.

1948

Q: When was the first television telecast in Boston?

A: WBZ television went on the air on June 9. After several hours of test patterns, newsman Arch MacDonald read news for fifteen minutes. Then at 6:30 P.M. MacDonald introduced a film of congratulations from Catholic, Episcopal, and Jewish leaders, followed by the *Kraft Television Theater* and other shows. During Boston's first day of television, more than one hundred thousand tuned in to watch.

1952

New *Boston Post* owner John Fox reversed the paper's longtime Democratic political stance to endorse Dwight Eisenhower for president.

An example of how Fox embarrassed the *Post* with his clumsy anticommunist campaigns occurred when Fox ordered a story criticizing the Boston Public Library for corrupting Boston schoolchildren by carrying the Russian-language newspapers *Pravda* and *Isvestia.* Advised that perhaps not one Boston schoolchild could read these papers in Russian, Fox insisted on printing the story anyway.

In the same year, Fox took $50,000 from Joseph P. Kennedy as a payment or a loan whose quid pro quo was support of John F. Kennedy for the U.S. Senate.

1955

W. Davis Taylor became publisher of the *Globe* on the death of his father, William O. Taylor. Davis Taylor hired Laurence Winship as the *Globe*'s editor.

1956

The *Post* closed its doors.

On June 9, 1948, more than 100,000 people saw Boston's first telecast by WBZ.

1957

Former *Post* publisher John Fox helped bring about the resignation of Eisenhower adviser Sherman Adams and the arrest of businessman Bernard Goldfine with accusations made in testimony before a House subcommittee. Fox was motivated by grudges stemming from a battle for a television channel and an investigation of Fox by the Internal Revenue Service.

1965

Thomas Winship became editor of the *Globe*.

1966

The *Globe* won its first Pulitzer Prize, for investigative reporting.

1967

The *Boston Globe* endorsed mayoral candidate Kevin White over antibusing advocate Louise Day Hicks. The *Globe* had not endorsed a candidate since 1896 but broke this tradition because it perceived Hicks as a representative of racist and segregationist policies.

1971

Q: What were the Pentagon Papers, and who published them?

A: The *Globe* followed the lead of the *New York Times* in publishing selections from the Pentagon Papers, the nickname of a forty-seven-volume secret history of American involvement in Vietnam prepared under the direction of Defense Secretary Robert McNamara.

One of the study's authors, Daniel Ellsberg of Cambridge, had leaked the first selections to the *Times,* which won a Pulitzer Prize for the publication. The *Globe* then tracked down Ellsberg, who was in hiding, and arranged to publish additional excerpts from the report. The *Globe* had been one of the first newspapers to oppose America's involvement in Vietnam, though it had endorsed Vietnam War apologist Hubert Humphrey for president in 1968.

In 1921, WBZ became the country's second commercial radio station and made its first telecast in 1948.

1973

The *Globe* was the first newspaper to call for President Nixon's resignation.

1975

The *Globe* won a Pulitzer Prize for coverage of the desegregation of Boston's schools.

1978

Q: How was the *Globe* embarrassed during the Carter presidency?

A: During the administration of Pres. Jimmy Carter a story in the *Globe* newsroom quoting Carter was jokingly headlined "More Mush from the Wimp." The *Globe* was extremely embarrassed when the headline was inadvertently printed.

1979

The *Globe* began to use computers to prepare news stories for print.

1984

The *Globe* won a Pulitzer for a series titled "Boston: The Race Factor."

1993

Q: How much did the New York Times Company pay to acquire the *Boston Globe*?

A: The New York Times Company bought Affiliated Publications, owner of the *Globe*, for $1.1 billion.

1998

In July, award-winning columnist and poet Patricia Smith of the *Globe* was asked to resign after evidence was found that she had made up characters and quotations in four of her columns. Despite rumors and accusations that columnist and media personality Mike Barnicle had done the same thing, and the discovery that a recent Barnicle column had used material by comedian George Carlin without attribution, Barnicle was not immediately asked to resign. Some supporters of Smith argued that Barnicle was receiving the benefit of a double standard, that Irish-American male Barnicle was getting lighter treatment than black female Smith. Further investigation by the *Globe* and other media uncovered at least three more instances of plagiarism and fabrication in Barnicle's work, and Barnicle was forced to resign a month after Smith.

*Boston's mounted finest meander down Boylston Street between a colonial burial
ground and Dunkin' Donuts.*

10

Crime and Punishment

The underside of a Puritan city

Mrs. Thatcher is doing for monetarism what the Boston Strangler did for door-to-door salesmen.
—DENIS (LORD) HEALEY, IN THE HOUSE OF COMMONS, 1979

CRIME HAS BEEN PRESENT in Boston from the beginning. In fact, as befits a city founded by men and women who believed in strict regulation of behavior, Boston has a history of innovation in both law enforcement and lawbreaking.

The nation's first police force was created in Boston, and the nation's first police strike took place here. The pirates who preyed on Boston's seagoing trade were sometimes depraved beyond belief—and they sometimes suffered extreme punishments as a result. In 1850, the murder of a socially prominent doctor by a highly regarded Harvard professor demonstrated that neither breeding nor education nor religion can eradicate the dark side of human nature.

Political crime and punishment too have flourished here. Abolitionists and fugitive slaves and their supporters and detractors have clashed violently in Boston. Famous controversies have arisen in Boston over the alleged crimes of anarchists, Vietnam War opponents, and battered women who may fear for their lives.

Sadly, but perhaps fittingly, Boston has recently become the site of the world's biggest art theft. The world's largest theft of cash, the 1950 Brinks robbery, took place in Boston. Naturally, the city is not proud of its famous stranglers and drunks. But the panorama of Boston crime has its fascination. For better and worse, Boston crime reflects the character of the city, the nation, and the human species.

1630

Ending drunkenness was one of the first items taken up by the Massachusetts Court of Assistants (which evolved into the general court or legislature). Punishments included fines, whipping, and "bilbowes," or shackles. Gov. John Winthrop discouraged the practice of drinking toasts.

1631

On April 12, the court established "watches" to be on duty during the night. The watch consisted of six men and a constable, unpaid and chosen by a draft system.

The court also outlawed the firing of guns at night: "If any person fire off a piece after the watch is set, he shall be fined forty shillings, or be whipped."

1632

Q: Who was Boston's first pirate?

A: Boston's first pirate was Dixey Bull, who was trading with Indians along the Maine coast when a French ship took his goods. Short of provisions, Bull searched unsuccessfully for the ship that had robbed him, plundering other vessels along the way. Bull then decided to rob trading stations on the New England coast. A Boston ship and several other New England vessels chased him, but Dixey Bull got away and did not return.

As ants cluster about the honey pot, so did pirates gather about Boston.

—JOHN JENNINGS, *BOSTON, CRADLE OF LIBERTY*

Numerous pirates and privateers started in Boston, preyed on Boston shipping, or were imprisoned or hanged in Boston. Privateers were seamen commissioned by one country to prey on the ships of another. Once a privateer started plundering ships, he often chose his victims without making fine discriminations. The following is a list of pirates and privateers who started out or ended up in Boston:

Dixey Bull	Edward Hull
Ned Low	Thomas Hawkins
John Quelch	James Gillam
William Kidd	Joseph Bradish
William Fly	Tee Wetherley
Thomas Tew	

1634

Q: Who built Boston's first stocks for punishing wrongdoers?
A: A carpenter named Palmer made the first stocks on the Boston Common. His bill for £1.13 was considered too high—and he was locked in the stocks as punishment.

1635

Boston's first prison was built on Prison Lane—today known as Court Street.

1636

The Court established wards to guard the peace during the day.

1637

Q: Who were the first murderers hanged in Boston?
A: On September 28, John Williams and William Schooler became the first Boston men to be hanged for murder.

1701

Members of the watch were required to carry a "watch hook," which served as identification and might be considered a precursor of the billy club.

1714

A jailkeeper noted that he had fourteen men and two women in prison. Debt was the crime of six of the prisoners, five were in for drinking, three for theft, one for adultery, and one for "buggary."

1719

Ned Low left Boston when his wife died and embarked on a career of piracy. During the next five years, Low plundered numerous ships and settlements around New England. Colorful tales of his cruelty abound:

> *They cut and whipped some and others they burnt with*
> *Matches between their Fingers to the bone to make them confess*
> *where their Money was.*
> —AMERICAN WEEKLY MERCURY, JUNE 13, 1723

Low's fate was uncertain. One rumor had it that his companions abandoned him on an uninhabited island. A more likely story claimed that he was hanged by the French at Martinique.

1783

On April 17 the legislature created the position of Inspector of Police, the first time the word "police" appeared in city records.

1798

Charles Bulfinch became superintendent of police, directing twenty watchmen and twelve constables.

No longer in use, Boston's Charles Street Jail welcomed numerous felons in its day.

1817

Q: Who was the first to use the insanity defense, and how did it work out?

A: After killing his wife in a bout of drunken violence, William McDonough became the first man in the United States to plead not guilty by reason of insanity. He was hanged.

1838

Boston created a force of "day police" who wore green badges.

1841

Q: Who has been called the first probation officer?

A: Fifty-seven-year-old shoemaker John Augustus was in court and saw a man who was charged with drunkenness. Augustus paid his bail and helped him to get sober, and three weeks later the judge was so impressed that he fined the man one cent. Augustus was so pleased with helping the man that he bailed out seventeen more people in 1841. In the next eighteen years he bailed out close to two thousand more people and assisted numerous other homeless children and prostitutes. Because of these actions, Augustus has been called the first probation officer.

1849

The nineteenth century's "murder of the century" took place on North Grove Street on November 23. Harvard professor John White Webster killed Dr. George Parkman—brother of famous historian Francis Parkman, and brother-in-law of Robert Gould Shaw, who would later die leading one of Massachusetts's black regiments in the Civil War—over a loan of some $2,000 that Webster was having difficulty repaying.

The prominence and social and intellectual standing of both killer and victim, and the killer's early denials and methods of attempting to conceal the facts, added to the sensationalism of the case. Webster was a respected professor of chemistry and geology who liked to entertain distinguished guests, including the poet Longfellow. Parkman at age sixty had retired from medicine and grown rich in real estate and banking and had donated land for the Massachusetts Medical College and endowed a professorship there.

I never had the remotest idea of injuring Dr. Parkman until the moment the blow was struck. Dr. Parkman was extremely severe and sharp-tongued . . . and I am irritable and passionate. . . . I have never acquired the control over my passions that I ought to have acquired early; and the consequence is—all this.
    —PROF. JOHN WHITE WEBSTER, AFTER BEING FOUND GUILTY

To hide his guilt, Webster had dismembered Parkman's body and attempted to burn it. But a janitor who suspected the truth found bones and led police to the evidence. When Webster was arrested he swallowed a strychnine pellet, but it failed to kill him.

Some sixty thousand people attended the twelve-day trial, beginning on March 12, 1850. The crowd gathered before dawn and tickets were handed out to help the police keep order. People were rotated in and out of the gallery at short intervals to allow more spectators to get a look.

On August 30, Webster was hanged.

Harvard history professor Simon Schama retold the story in his 1995 novel, *Dead Certainties.*

1851

Boston police marshal Francis Tukey captured fugitive slave Thomas Sims and returned him to slavery. Tukey's efforts in the Sims case contributed to the eventual loss of his position.

1853

Harbor police were organized to guard ships at anchor. The harbor police carried revolvers.

1854

Day police and the night watch were joined together to create the Boston Police Department, with eight stations scattered through the city and a force of some 250 men. The new police department immediately had to deal with a major civil disturbance, the agitation surrounding the trial of fugitive slave Anthony Burns.

1855

The Boston police traded in their watch hooks for fourteen-inch billy clubs.

1885

Republicans in the state legislature passed a bill taking control of the Boston police force from the mayor and giving it to the Republican governor. Control of the police remained with the governor until 1962, when it was given back to the mayor of Boston.

1898

The Massachusetts legislature adopted the electric chair as the state's method of execution and abolished hanging.

1908

Three men robbed a Jamaica Plain bar and were chased to Forest Hills Cemetery by police. They held off three hundred police for two days, wounding nine people before one robber was killed and the others captured.

1920

Q: What crime were Nicola Sacco and Bartolomeo Vanzetti charged with?

A: On April 15 in South Braintree, the paymaster of the Slater and Morrill shoe factory and his bodyguard were shot to death and the factory's payroll of $15,777 was stolen. Witnesses reported that the crime was committed by two dark-skinned foreigners.

A few weeks later police in Bridgewater were investigating a failed robbery in which Bridgewater police chief Michael Stewart suspected "an out-of-town band of Russians." He also suspected a local man, Michael Boda. When Boda was spotted with a group of friends, police were called. The group scattered, and police intercepted a streetcar that some members of the group had boarded and arrested two dark foreigners, Nicola Sacco and Bartolomeo Vanzetti.

The men were anarchists, active as speechmakers and demonstrators against capitalism. Both carried guns when they were arrested, and both lied about the guns and about their recent activities.

These facts, and the testimony of a questionable weapons expert that the bullets used in the murder matched Sacco's gun, constituted the prosecution's primary case. The prejudices of the prosecution and the presiding judge were palpable. "I will crucify those damned God-hating radicals," district attorney Fred Katzmann said. After the trial, Judge Webster Thayer remarked, "Did you see what I did to those anarchist bastards?"

1921

On July 14, Judge Thayer sentenced Sacco and Vanzetti to death. Demonstrations against the verdict were held around the world. A bomb exploded at the home of one of the jurors, and Judge Thayer was put under guard. Two bombs exploded in Paris, where twenty-eight thousand police and soldiers kept crowds from storming the American embassy. Picketers marched around the State House in Boston. A petition with more than 474,000 names was presented to the governor. H. G. Wells, George Bernard Shaw, and John dos Passos were among those protesting the verdict.

Gov. Alvan T. Fuller appointed a committee chaired by Harvard president Abbot Lawrence Lowell to consider the verdict. The committee concluded that the trial had been fair.

1927

Sacco and Vanzetti were executed by electric chair on August 23. Vanzetti's comments after his final appeal was denied proved to be justifiably famous:

> *If it had not been for these thing, I might have live out my life talking at street corners to scorning men. I might have die, unmarked, unknown, a failure. This is our career and our triumph. Never in our full life could we hope to do such work for tolerance, for justice, for man's understanding of man as we do now by accident. Our words—our lives—our pains—nothing! The taking of our lives—lives of a good shoemaker and a poor fish peddler—all! That last moment belongs to us. That agony is our triumph.*

1935

Abraham Faber and brothers Murton and Irving Millen were executed in the electric chair for four murders committed during a series of holdups.

1950

Q: What was the biggest cash robbery in history?

A: On January 17, seven men wearing identical rubber masks and black chauffeur's hats broke into the offices of the Brinks security company at the corner of Commercial and Prince Streets in Boston. They tied up the Brinks employees and taped their mouths shut, and they left with $1.2 million in cash and another $1.5 million in securities, checks, and money orders.

The cash represented more than twice as much as anyone had taken in a single robbery before.

On January 6, 1956, with only eleven days remaining until the statute of limitations expired and the Brinks robbers could no longer be prosecuted, a petty thief named "Specs" O'Keefe confessed to the FBI, which had spent nearly $29 million on the investigation. With O'Keefe's confession in hand, another eight men were arrested, convicted, and sent to Walpole State Prison.

1962

From June 1962 to January 1964 the Boston Strangler raped and murdered thirteen women. He apparently talked his way into apartments then brutally killed their occupants, lone women ranging in age from nineteen to eighty-five. He left their stockings tied in bows under their chins.

Brinks, Inc., achieved a dubious distinction when crooks took $2.7 million from its Boston office in 1950.

Albert Desalvo was arrested for breaking and entering and then confined to Bridgewater State Mental Hospital, where he confessed the strangler's crimes to fellow inmate and killer George Nassar. Nassar alerted his lawyer, F. Lee Bailey, who questioned Desalvo and became convinced he was the Boston Strangler.

Desalvo was never formally charged with the Boston Strangler murders. He was instead convicted of a series of unrelated rapes. He was stabbed to death in his cell at Walpole State Prison in 1973.

1970

Q: What crime was committed by a group of robbers that included two recent Brandeis graduates?

A: Two women and three men robbed an Allston branch of the State Street Bank, getting away with some $26,000. A police officer and father of nine children, Walter Schroeder, was shot and killed in the parking lot.

The robbers were Katherine Ann Power, Susan Saxe, William Gilday, Stanley Bond, and Richard Valeri. The two women had just graduated from Brandeis University, and the avowed purpose of the robbery was to raise money for activities intended to put an end to the Vietnam War.

Saxe, Bond, and Valeri went into the bank, where shots were fired, but nobody was hurt. Gilday, in the parking lot with the first getaway car, shot Schroeder. Power was waiting blocks away with a second getaway car.

The three men were caught quickly, one at a time, and Gilday was sentenced to life imprisonment for the murder. Susan Saxe surrendered in 1976, after the war in Vietnam had ended.

Power evaded capture for twenty-three years and finally turned herself in in 1993. She was sentenced to eight to twelve years in prison, plus twenty years probation, and forbidden to profit from telling the story of the crime. The Supreme Court ruled that this provision did not violate Power's right to free speech, because she had not been forbidden to tell her story but only to profit from the telling. In 1997 Power was up for parole, but she apologized for her crimes and withdrew her parole application.

1974

A Boston grand jury indicted Dr. Kenneth Edelin for manslaughter for performing an abortion on a woman in her twentieth to twenty-fourth week of pregnancy and allegedly allowing a living baby to die. The case, which resulted in part from investigations initiated by Boston city councilor Albert "Dapper" O'Neill, state representative and later mayor Ray Flynn, and district attorney Newman Flanagan, became a symbol in the conflict between supporters of a woman's right to choose her reproductive course and proponents of the right to life of the fetus or baby after conception. A jury found Edelin guilty and the judge sentenced him to one year of probation, pending his appeal. The Massachusetts Supreme Judicial Court reversed Edelin's conviction.

1989

On October 23, Charles "Chuck" Stuart shot and killed his pregnant wife, Carol DiMaiti Stuart, and wounded himself to make the killing appear to be a robbery by an African American in Boston's Mission Hill neighborhood. For days the scheme worked. Police stopped and searched hundreds of black men and finally arrested a man, William Bennett, who seemed to them a likely suspect. From his hospital bed, Stuart claimed to identify Bennett.

Stuart and his wife were going home from a childbirth class at Brigham and Women's Hospital when the shootings took place. Two of the major flaws in Stuart's plan were that he wounded himself in the abdomen much more severely than he had meant to, and that he was depending on his younger brother, to whom he handed off a bag containing jewelry and the gun, to keep his mouth shut, even after learning that his wife had been murdered.

Other flaws included the facts that the Stuarts started out in the wrong direction for a couple returning to a home in Reading, and that Stuart had previously talked to at least three people about the possibility of killing his wife.

Stuart was already making more than $100,000 as manager of a Boston fur retailer, not bad for a man without a college degree. Reportedly, he was interested in Debbie Allen, a coworker, and may have felt that she represented a step up socially, even though his wife was a lawyer with degrees from Boston College and Suffolk Law School. Stuart hoped to open a restaurant, and his wife's life was insured for more than $180,000.

On January 4, 1990, Stuart apparently killed himself by jumping off the Tobin Bridge into the freezing Mystic River.

Considering the flaws in Stuart's crime, the police, newspaper, and public responses to his story about being robbed by an African American on Mission Hill have been justifiably condemned. The DiMaiti family established a foundation in their daughter's name to award scholarships to deserving youth from the Mission Hill neighborhood. In the first year, donations poured in.

1990

Q: How did thieves steal $200 million worth of paintings?
A: On March 18, two men dressed in police uniforms talked guards at the Isabella Stewart Gardner Museum into letting them in. They tied up the guards with electrical tape, disabled the museum's security system, and worked for two hours removing objects worth at least $200 million.

Stolen paintings and objects were:

The Concert, Jan Vermeer, one of only thirty-two Vermeers in existence
A Lady and Gentleman in Black, Rembrandt
The Storm on the Sea of Galilee, Rembrandt—his only seascape
Self-Portrait, Rembrandt
Landscape with an Obelisk, Govaert Flinck (a pupil of Rembrandt)
Chez Tortoni, Manet
Five paintings by Degas
A Shang Dynasty bronze beaker (the museum's oldest object, dating from ca. 1200 B.C.)

None of the objects was insured, because insurance would have been too expensive. Auction houses Christie's and Sotheby's offered a $1 million reward. The only art theft in history to rival this one

This U-Haul parked at the Isabella Stewart Gardner Museum probably was not used by the thieves who took $200 million worth of paintings in 1990.

was the theft of Leonardo's *Mona Lisa* from the Louvre in 1911. That painting was returned two years later.

1992

Q: Who were the Framingham Eight?

A: On February 14, 1992, the legal team of the Task Force on Battered Women and Self-Defense submitted eight petitions for commutation to Governor Weld. The Framingham Eight were eight women imprisoned in Framingham State Prison for killing husbands or boyfriends who had repeatedly beaten and abused them.

In 1996, women's rights advocates demonstrated at the State House asking Gov. William Weld to pardon Patricia Hennessy, the final member of the Framingham Eight to remain in prison. Freed Framingham Eight members Elaine Hyde and Eugenia Moore took part in the demonstration.

1994

The Reverend Accelynne Williams died of a heart attack when thirteen heavily armed Boston police burst into his apartment in search of guns and drugs. Williams lived on the second floor; the apartment the police really wanted to raid was on the third.

1996

On June 25, Harvard University investigator Richard W. Mederos found $500,000 worth of books and artwork cut out of books at the apartment of Jose Torres-Carbonnel, along with evidence that another $250,000 worth had already been shipped to Spain. Torres had an airline ticket and was planning to leave for Spain that day.

1997

Operation Cease Fire, a Boston program designed to combat gang violence, received an Innovations in American Government Award, administered by the John F. Kennedy School of Government in Cambridge and sponsored by the Ford Foundation.

Boston Marathon legend Bill Rodgers wore his trademark cap to New York in 1980.

11

Wait Till Next Year

America's greatest sports town

> *I like to play baseball, but this is a business for me and I can't be governed by sentiment.*
> —JIMMY COLLINS, ON JUMPING FROM THE BEANEATERS
> TO THE PILGRIMS FOR $4,000 A YEAR

BOSTON SPORTS FANATICS BOAST that they are the greatest fans in the greatest sports town in America. They claim to be the most knowledgeable fans, and to have, if not the most successful amateur and professional organizations and events, at least the teams and events with the most noble traditions.

Such claims, of course, are overblown and chauvinistic. But they have some basis in fact.

Boston's major professional sports teams, the Red Sox, Celtics, Bruins, and Patriots, have great and winning traditions. Other professional sports teams have passed through or are currently seeking to establish themselves in Boston. Tennis great Martina Navratilova played for the Boston Lobsters. Boston's Major League Soccer team, the Revolution, featured colorful Olympic star Alexi Lalas and outstanding goalkeeper Walter Zenga. The New England Blizzard

201

fought to establish themselves in the already defunct Women's Basketball League.

Boston's amateur sports scene is also diverse and enthusiastic. The annual Beanpot Hockey Tournament establishes the city's college hockey champion among competitors Harvard, Boston College, Boston University, and Northeastern, teams that frequently compete for national championships and contribute many players to the National Hockey League. The Head of the Charles Regatta is the world's largest rowing event. The Boston Marathon is arguably the world's premier long-distance footrace.

The history and lore of Boston sports can and do fill many books. For the purposes of the present book, we have focused on the city's oldest and most storied sports team—the Red Sox, the city's and the world's most successful professional team—the Celtics, and our most glamorous event that is still at least open to amateurs—the Boston marathon.

The Boston Marathon

1897

Q: When was the first Boston Marathon run?

A: The first Boston Marathon started at Metcalfe's Mill in Ashland, Massachusetts, at 12:19 P.M. on April 19, 1897, the anniversary of Paul Revere's 1775 ride. It was not the first marathon run in the United States. That honor belonged to a race that had been run six months earlier from Stamford, Connecticut, to Columbus Circle in New York.

The field for the first Boston Marathon included just fifteen runners, six of them from New York. Most wore heavy boots and toreador pants. The race was won by New Yorker John J. McDermott despite an unfortunate mishap. On Massachusetts Avenue, McDermott ran into the middle of a funeral procession, causing two of the funeral's newfangled electric cars to stall. Nevertheless, McDermott won the race by 7 minutes over the second-place finisher. The first Boston Marathon was run at a distance of 24.5 miles, which McDermott ran in 2 hours, 55 minutes, 10 seconds.

1898

Twenty-two-year-old Boston College student Ronald McDonald won the second Boston Marathon (still at 24.5 miles) in 2 hours, 42 minutes.

1901

Q: What was the first scandal in Boston Marathon history?

A: The first scandal in Boston Marathon history arose when rumors spread that Ronald McDonald, who collapsed at Cleveland Circle, had been handed a chloroformed sponge with which to wipe his face. Canadian James Caffrey, who had also won the year before, became the first repeat winner of the event.

1905

Fred Lorz of New York won in Boston, just a year after he had been disqualified from the Olympic marathon after allegedly traversing thirteen miles of the course in the back seat of an automobile.

1909

Impostor Howard Pearce dropped out after eight miles, accepted a ride, and stepped back on the course to run the final mile before a cheering crowd.

1918

Q: What event was held in place of the marathon?

A: Due to World War I, the marathon was canceled. Instead of the marathon, a military relay race was won by a ten-man team from Fort Devens.

1917

Freddy Merchant, a serious contender in the race, accepted a brief ride that helped him to a fifth-place finish before his disqualification.

1923

Clarence DeMar won the marathon, the second of his seven Boston victories, despite a training incident in which he was bitten by a dog and punched by the dog's owner. The bite became infected, but DeMar recovered in time to win the race.

1924

This year officials tried to adjust the Boston Marathon's distance to the standard 26 miles, 385 yards, but they fell 176 yards short, and contestants ran 26 miles, 209 yards until officials finally got it right in 1927.

1946

Q: Which marathon winner ran the race to help feed his country-men?

A: The winner this year was Stylianos Kyriakides, a Greek who ran the race to publicize postwar famine in his native country. It worked. Kyriakides's victory focused attention on his country and led to a flood of aid.

1947

Yun Bok Suh of Korea won despite a broken shoelace and a spill caused by a fox terrier on the course. His trip to Boston had been partially financed by American soldiers in Korea.

1950

Q: What nickname was given to the Korean winner?

A: Koreans swept the first three places, led by Kee Yong Ham, who was nicknamed "Swift Premium" by the press.

1953

Q: What embarrassing error led to three course records being thrown out?

A: Due to construction, the course was accidentally shortened to 25 miles, 938 yards, and the error wasn't discovered and corrected until after the 1956 race. Course records set in 1953, 1955, and 1956 had to be discounted.

1961

Q: What dog succeeded in affecting the outcome of the race where a fellow canine had failed in 1923?

A: A black mongrel dog played a major role in the race this year. John "the Younger" Kelley was tripped by the dog at the sixteen-mile mark, and Kelley ended up losing the race by less than half a minute. Also seriously affected by the incident was runner Jim Norris, who was running with the leaders when Kelley was knocked down. Norris stopped to help Kelley up. Eino Oksanen of Finland won the race, the second of three Boston wins for "the Ox."

John Kelley "the Younger" ended up finishing second at Boston five times. He is not related to marathon legend John Kelley "the Elder," who finished second seven times and won the race twice.

1965

Japanese runners took five of the first six places. Morio Sheigematsu finished first.

1966

Roberta Gibb ran unofficially, becoming the first woman to run in the marathon and the first woman to finish.

Japanese runners swept the first four places, led by winner Kenji Kimihara.

1967

Q: Who was the first woman to run Boston with a number, and what embarrassing incident occurred?

A: Twenty-year-old Kathy Switzer of Syracuse University entered the race as K. Switzer and received a number. About two miles into the race she was spotted by runner and Boston Marathon legend Jock Semple who pushed her and tried to rip her number off. Semple was restrained by Switzer's friend Arnie Briggs and boyfriend, Tom Miller, and she went on to finish the race.

1968

Ambrose Burfoot of Connecticut won the race in 2 hours, 22 minutes, 17 seconds.

1969

The field topped the thousand mark for the first time as 1,150 runners started the marathon.

1970

Wheelchair marathoner Eugene Roberts, racing unofficially, finished in 7 hours.

1972

Women were officially allowed to race for the first time. Nina Kuscsik became the first official women's champion in a time of 3 hours, 10 minutes, 26 seconds. Kuscsik had taken up running as a way to get through a difficult divorce, and in this race she beat her former husband by 11 minutes.

1974

Q: Who was the smallest person ever to win a Boston Marathon title?

A: The women's winner, Miki Gorman, weighed eighty-nine pounds. Her time was 2 hours, 47 minutes, 11 seconds.

1975

Bob Hall became the first official wheelchair entrant and finished in 2 hours, 58 minutes.

Hometown hero Bill Rodgers, probably the runner most responsible for creating the marathon boom, upset a field of 2,041 by completing the race in a course and American record of 2 hours, 9 minutes, 55 seconds. Rodgers stopped five times during the race—four times for water and once to tie his shoelace.

1976

Q: What nickname was given to the 1976 race?

A: It was so hot that thousands of spectators from homes along the route turned welcomed garden hoses on the runners. So the 1976 Boston Marathon was nicknamed "the Run for the Hoses."

1980

Impostor Rosie Ruiz jumped in at the twenty-five-mile mark and crossed the finish line 3 minutes before the legitimate women's winner, Jacqueline Gareau.

1982

Alberto Salazar dueled Dick Beardley to the finish, winning by 2 seconds.

1986

Prize money was paid to the top fifteen men's and women's finishers for the first time.

1987

John Hancock Financial Services Corporation committed $10 million to sponsor the race over the following ten years.

1988

Ibrahim Hussein won the closest marathon ever by a 1-second margin. This was the first time the race had been won by a black man.

1993

Kenyan Cosmas Ndeti began a string of three lucrative wins. His comment: "On my farm I am gathering Mercedes-Benz cars to go with my water buffalo. Pretty soon I think I must get my driver's license."

1996

An open division was established for the one hundredth running of the marathon. Entries were determined by lottery to create the largest field ever to run a marathon.

The Boston Red Sox

1876

Q: What were the first two names of the team that is now the Atlanta Braves?

A: The Boston Red Stockings, soon to be renamed the Beaneaters (and precursors of today's Atlanta Braves), were charter members of the newly formed National League.

1898

The Beaneaters won the National League pennant for the eighth time in twenty-two years. Famous Beaneaters players included third baseman Jimmy Collins and outfielder Hugh Duffy.

1900–1901

Entrepreneur Byron Bancroft "Ban" Johnson changed the name of his Western Association to the "American League" and a year later declared it a second major league. The Boston Pilgrims, later to become the Red Sox, were a charter member of the American League.

At age thirty-four, Cy Young jumped from St. Louis to the Pilgrims for $3,500. He finished the 1901 season with 33 wins, 10 losses (in a year when the team only played 138 games).

The Pilgrims played at the Huntington Avenue Grounds, with a seating capacity of seven thousand. Standing room was roped off in the outfield when needed.

1902

Cy Young's record plunged to 32–11.

1903

Q: Who was the Red Sox's (actually Pilgrims') first home-run king?

A: Buck Freeman became the first Boston player to lead the AL in homers. He smashed 13. At age thirty-six, Cy Young slumped to 28–9.

Q: During the first World Series, how did Cy Young help out before the game?

A: The first World Series pitted the Pilgrims against the Pittsburgh Pirates and star shortstop Honus Wagner. The game drew sixteen thousand fans—so many that Cy Young and some of his teammates were drafted to help sell tickets before the game. Young then pitched the first game and lost it, 7–3.

Fortunately for Boston, the series was scheduled to be won by the first team to win five of nine games, a format that was tried again in three more series from 1919 to 1921. All other World Series have been a best-of-seven series.

The Pirates had lost one starting pitcher to a mental breakdown late in the season, and another Pirates starter developed arm trouble during the series. So one man, Deacon Phillippe, did much of the pitching for Pittsburgh. After Phillippe became understandably exhausted, Boston clinched the series with a 3–0 win in the eighth game. Phillippe's record of 44 innings pitched in the series is unlikely to be broken. Bill Dinneen was the winning pitcher for Boston.

1904

Q: Why was there no World Series this year?

A: Boston beat the New York Highlanders 3–2 on the last day of the season to clinch the pennant. But John McGraw and his New York Giants refused to play a World Series against the upstart American League.

The glassed-in Six Hundred Club, a recent addition to Fenway Park, has uglified the place and altered its wind currents.

On May 5, 1904, thirty-seven-year-old Cy Young pitched the first perfect game of the twentieth century.

1907

Now officially known as the Red Sox, the team lost its manager when thirty-four-year-old Chick Stahl died during spring training. Cy Young managed for seven games. Former Chicago Cubs scout George Huff took over for eight games. First baseman Bob Unglaub managed the next twenty-eight, losing twenty. Finally Deacon McGuire took over for the rest of the season, lifting the team one step out of the cellar, up to seventh place. The first Red Sox season will probably never be equaled for spring misfortunes or for managerial musical chairs.

1908

Cy Young, now forty-one, went a meager 21–11 with a no-hitter against New York. When the season ended, the Sox sold him to

Cleveland for $12,500. Those who feel the 1997 Red Sox were ungrateful to Roger Clemens should take note.

1910

Q: How many Red Sox have led the league in homers?
A: Jake Stahl led the league with 10 homers to become the Red Sox's second home-run king. Through the 1998 season the Red Sox had seventeen league-leading home-run hitters.

1912

On April 20 the Red Sox beat the Yankees 7–6 in the first game ever played at Fenway Park. Boston mayor and grandfather of JFK John F. "Honey Fitz" Fitzgerald threw out the first ball at the new park. The field was muddy on opening day, and the Red Sox won despite committing 7 errors.

Fenway's first homer was hit on April 26 by backup first baseman Hugh Bradley.

Neither a video scoreboard nor giant Coke bottles scaling a light tower can negate Fenway Park's status as a shrine of baseball.

Led by Smoky Joe Wood and his 34–5 record, the Sox won the pennant with ease in their first Fenway season. Tris Speaker hit .383, and his 10 homers tied him for the league lead.

Boston beat the Giants in the last inning of the eighth game of the series. The second game had been a 6–6 tie, called when it got too dark to finish.

1913

In spring training, Smoky Joe Wood slipped while fielding a bunt, broke his thumb, and was never the same pitcher again.

1914

The Federal League made a brief appearance, attempting to become a third major league. Despite its quick demise, it had two major effects on Boston baseball history.

Tris Speaker used the leverage of the competition with the new league to negotiate a raise from $9,000 to $36,000. There were hard feelings, and management cut him back to $9,000 when the new league folded. Speaker was traded to Cleveland in 1916.

Meanwhile, the Baltimore Orioles of the International League, an independent team, were losing money due to Federal League competition. So they sold three young players to the Red Sox. One of them was nineteen-year-old first-year pitcher George Herman "Babe" Ruth.

Dutch Leonard posted the lowest earned-run average in history, 1.01.

1915

Q: What was Babe Ruth's record for the Sox in 1915?
A: Ruth went 18–8, hit .315, and had 4 homers, just 3 short of the league leader.

The Sox beat the Phillies in the World Series. The Boston games were played at Braves Field instead of Fenway Park because Braves Field had more seats. Ruth made only one appearance, pinch-hitting in the opener and grounding out.

1916

The Sox won the pennant again. Ruth went 23–12 with a 1.75 ERA. The team set a record for fewest errors and led the league in fielding percentage, the first of six consecutive fielding titles. The Sox beat the Dodgers in five games in the series.

In the offseason, thirty-six-year-old Harry Frazee bought the team.

1918

Q: Who tied for the league lead in homers for the 1918 Red Sox?
A: The Red Sox won their fourth pennant—and fourth World Series—in seven years. The season was shortened due to World War I; the Sox played 126 games. Ruth went 13–7, but he had begun playing the outfield. In 317 at-bats he hit .300 and tied for the league lead in homers with 11, the first of 12 home-run titles.

In December, Harry Frazee sold Ernie Shore, Duffy Lewis, and Dutch Leonard to the Yankees for $15,000 and four lesser players.

1919

Frazee sold star pitcher Carl Mays to the Yankees for $40,000. Playing mostly outfield for the Sox, Ruth shattered the home-run record, raising it from 16 to 29.

Q: What did the Red Sox owner get for Babe Ruth?
A: Strapped for money, Frazee sold Ruth to the Yankees on December 26 for $125,000 and a $300,000 personal loan.

1923

Frazee sold Herb Pennock to the Yankees. In previous years he had sold eventual Hall of Famers Waite Hoyt and Joe Dugan to New York, along with numerous other excellent players.

On September 7, Sox pitcher Howard Ehmke threw a no-hitter against the Philadelphia Athletics. In his next start on September 11 against the Yankees, Ehmke threw a one-hitter. The only hit was a bad-hop single that could easily have been scored an error that would have made Ehmke the first pitcher to throw two consecutive no-hitters.

In July, Harry Frazee sold the Sox to Bob Quinn.

The Yankees won the World Series with eleven former Red Sox, including Ruth, on their roster.

1925

Frazee finally had a hit show on Broadway, *No, No, Nanette.*

1932

The Sox had their worst record ever, 42–111, and their worst attendance ever, 182,150.

1933

Bob Quinn sold the team to thirty-year-old Thomas Austin Yawkey.

In December, Yawkey purchased Lefty Grove from Connie Mack's Philadelphia Athletics.

1934

Yawkey bought pitcher Wes Ferrell from Cleveland. He also bought shortstop Joe Cronin from Clark Griffith's Washington Senators for $250,000. Griffith sold Cronin despite the fact that Cronin was also manager of the team—and Griffith's son-in-law.

1935

Yawkey bought Jimmy Foxx from Connie Mack. Foxx had hit 58 homers in 1932.

1936

Q: Who discovered Ted Williams?
A: On a trip to San Diego, Eddie Collins observed the unique talent, concentration, and ambition of seventeen-year-old Ted Williams.

1938

Foxx hit .349 with 50 homers and 175 runs batted in and became Boston's first winner of the Most Valuable Player award. The Sox outhit the Yanks .299 to .274 but still finished 9½ games behind them.

1939

Rookie outfielder Ted Williams hit .327 with 31 homers and 145 RBIs.

1941

Boston finished second, 17 games behind the Yankees who were led by Joe DiMaggio and his 56-game hitting streak, which ended July 17. But for the rest of the season, fans watched Ted Williams chase a magic batting average of .400 or better.

On the last day of the season, with a double-header scheduled in Philadelphia, Williams was hitting .3995, which would have been rounded off to give him an official average of exactly .400. Manager Joe Cronin offered to let him sit out the double-header. But Williams refused. He went 6 for 8 to end up at .406. Nobody has hit .400 since.

Q: Who won the MVP award in 1941?

A: Amazingly, DiMaggio won the MVP award that year, in spite of Williams's .406 average with 37 home runs. Considering DiMaggio's fielding, grace, and leadership and his team's success, there were few complaints.

1942

Ted Williams won the triple crown, leading the league in batting at .356, homers with 36, and RBIs with 137. When Yankee second baseman Joe Gordon was named MVP, there were quite a few complaints. The Sox finished second to the Yankees once again.

1946

Williams returned from three years in the marines to lead the Sox to 104 wins and a pennant. But the Cardinals beat the Sox in the seventh game of a memorable World Series. Williams was named league MVP.

1947

The Sox dropped to third place, but Williams won his second triple crown with a .343 average, 32 homers, and 114 RBIs. He lost the MVP by one vote to Joe DiMaggio. Williams would have won it if Boston sportswriter Mel Webb, who was feuding with Williams, had given him even as much as a tenth-place vote.

Q: When was the first Fenway Park night game?
A: The first evening game was played at Fenway Park on June 13, 1947.

1948

After the regular season ended with the Sox and Indians tied for first place at 96–58, a one-game playoff was held at Fenway Park. Sox manager Joe McCarthy made a controversial decision to start thirty-six-year-old Denny Galehouse, whose record that year was 8–8, because his three best pitchers were tired. The strategy didn't work as the Indians won the game and the pennant, 8–3. The Boston Braves won the National League pennant. Boston fans were bitterly disappointed that they had just missed having an all-Boston World Series.

1949

The Sox arrived in New York in October for the season's final two games. Going into the short series, Boston led the Yankees by one game. But the Sox lost two hard-fought games, 5–4 and 5–3. For the second time a pennant had been decided in a Boston–New York battle on the last day of the season.

Williams won the MVP award.

1950

Boston finished with a team average of .302 and scored 113 more runs than the first-place Yankees, but the Sox finished third in the division.

1953

On June 18 the Sox scored a record 17 runs in the seventh inning against the Tigers. Outfielder Gene Stephens became the only player to have three hits in one inning.

Q: How many missions did Ted Williams fly in Korea?
A: Ted Williams returned late in the season after flying thirty-nine missions in Korea. Once his plane was hit and nearly downed. He returned to appear in thirty-seven games in which he hit .407 with 13 homers.

1954

The thirty-five-year-old Williams, who hadn't played much baseball in four years due to a tour of duty in Korea, broke his collarbone on the first day of spring training. When he returned to the lineup in a double header against the Tigers on May 16, he went 8-for-9.

1957

Q: Who was the oldest batting champion?
A: At age thirty-nine, Williams became the oldest batting champion, hitting .388.

1958

Q: Who was the first to win the batting championship at age forty?
A: Surprise, Williams—age forty—won the batting title again, though with a modest .328 average.

1959

Elijah "Pumpsie" Green belatedly became the Red Sox's first black player.

1960

At the age of forty-two, Williams hit .316 with 29 homers in 310 at-bats. In the last home game of the season, which was to be Ted's final game, he hit his 521st home run in his final visit to the plate.

1965

Tony Conigliaro hit 32 home runs and became the youngest man ever to lead the league in homers.

1967

Carl Yastrzemski, a.k.a. Yaz, won the triple crown with a .326 average, 44 home runs, and 121 RBIs. In a tight four-team pennant race, Yaz had 23 hits in his last 44 at-bats, and the Sox won the pennant on the last day in what has come to be called the "Impossible Dream" season. But Lou Brock, Roger Maris, and pitcher Bob Gibson led the Cardinals to a 4–3 World Series victory.

Yaz won the MVP award.

Star pitcher Jim Lonborg injured his left knee in a skiing accident near Lake Tahoe on December 23 and never pitched well again.

1972

A brief strike shortened the season, and the Red Sox lost the division title after Hall of Fame shortstop and base stealer Luis Aparicio fell down rounding third base and tried to get back to the base where Yaz had just arrived. It was the final series of the season, and the Sox lost the division to their opponent in that game—the Detroit Tigers—by half a game.

1975

Q: Who was the first player to win both the Rookie of the Year and MVP awards in the same year?

A: Fred Lynn became the first player to win both Rookie of the Year and MVP honors.

Boston won its division by 4½ games and swept Oakland in the League Championship Series.

The Sox played Cincinnati in the World Series. That series has been called the best ever, and the sixth game was perceived by many to have been the greatest game ever played.

Fred Lynn opened the scoring in the sixth game with a 3-run homer. But the Reds led 6–3 in the eighth when Boston's Bernie Carbo tied the game with another 3-run shot. In the bottom of the ninth George Foster threw out Boston's Denny Doyle trying to score on Lynn's fly, and the game went to extra innings. In the top of the eleventh inning, Dwight Evans robbed Joe Morgan of a homer with a spectacular catch and doubled up famous baseball father Ken Griffey. But in the bottom of the twelfth Carlton Fisk hit a long, high drive down the left-field line that would end the game if it stayed fair. Fisk bounced toward first waving his arms, trying to coax the ball fair. It worked, and the play and resulting celebration remain one of the most famous scenes in baseball history.

The seventh game seemed anticlimactic. The Sox lost, 4–3. Their last world championship was in 1918.

1977

The Sox won 97 games but finished tied with Baltimore, 2½ games behind the Yankees.

1978

The Red Sox led the Yankees by 14 games in July. But Boston lost 14 of 17 in early September, while the New York club was playing awesome ball. The Yankees took a 3½-game lead in September, but the Sox came back, winning 11 of their last 13. Boston and New York finished the season 99–63.

Bucky Dent's 3-run homer in the seventh led the Yankees to a 5–4 victory in the playoff game.

1981

Q: How did Carlton Fisk leave the Sox?

A: Carlton Fisk's contract was accidentally mailed too late, and the error allowed him to become a free agent. He signed with the White Sox.

1983

Wade Boggs won his first AL batting title with a .361 average.

Carl Yastrzemski retired in 1983. He is the only American Leaguer to have more than 400 homers (452) as well as more than 3,000 hits (3,419).

1984

Newcomer Roger Clemens went 9–4 before hurting his arm in August. He struggled through the next year with arm trouble as well.

1986

Clemens went 24–4. He set a major league record on April 29 when he struck out 20 Mariners in one game. Clemens won both the Cy Young and MVP awards.

Boggs won his third batting title, hitting .357.

Jim Rice hit .324 with 110 RBIs.

Bill Buckner knocked in 102 runs, Dwight Evans 97, and Don Baylor 94.

The Red Sox led the Mets in the World Series 3–2 going into the sixth game. In the tenth inning of that game, the Sox took a 5–3 lead and appeared on the verge of their first championship since 1918.

Q: Who hit the ball that went through Bill Buckner's legs?
A: Mookie Wilson. Calvin Schiraldi retired the first two Mets in the bottom of the tenth then allowed 3 straight singles, making the score 5–4. Facing Mookie Wilson, Bob Stanley threw a wild pitch that tied the game. Then Wilson hit a bouncer toward Bill Buckner at first. It should have ended the inning easily, but instead it went through Buckner's legs and the winning run scored.

The Red Sox took a 3–0 lead in the seventh game, but the Mets came back to win the Series with an 8–5 victory.

1987

Clemens, 20–9 with 7 shutouts, won his second consecutive Cy Young award.

1988

Joe Morgan replaced John McNamara as manager after the all-star break, and the Red Sox won 12 in a row to get back in the race. In late September the Sox took 5 of 7 from the Yankees and won the division. But the Sox were swept by Oakland in the League Championship Series.

1990

The Red Sox ran away with the Eastern Division title but lost the American League Championship Series to the Oakland A's in four straight games.

1995

The Red Sox won the American League Eastern Division title just one year after hiring Massachusetts-born Dan Duquette away from the Montreal Expos to be the team's general manager.

Slugging first baseman Mo Vaughn won the American League MVP in a close vote over Cleveland's Albert Belle.

1996

Although hard-hitting and slick-fielding shortstop Nomar Garciaparra won the Rookie of the Year award, the Red Sox allowed 114 unearned runs for the season to lead the league and suffered their highest total in this category since 1934.

Boston rock band Slide released its first CD, titled *Forgiving Buckner,* commemorating the play that had extended Game 6 of the 1986 World Series.

In December, Roger Clemens, winner of three Cy Young awards as best pitcher in the league for the Red Sox and the only pitcher to strike out 20 hitters in one game twice, signed a three-year

$24.75 million contract to pitch for the Toronto Blue Jays. A sure Hall of Famer, Clemens would go on to win Cy Young awards in 1997 and 1998.

1998

In the midst of protracted contract negotiations during the off-season, slugger Mo Vaughn flipped his truck after hitting an empty vehicle parked in the breakdown lane during a rainstorm. Vaughn was returning after midnight from a visit to the Foxy Lady night-club in Providence, Rhode Island. He was acquitted of drunk driving charges, but rumors that the Sox had hired detectives to check up on Mo's private life made contract talks even more dicey. Besides hitting homers and visiting the Foxy Lady, Vaughn was known for his work on behalf of Boston-area ghetto youth. He finally signed a contract to play for the California Angels.

The Boston Celtics

1946

Walter Brown and other arena owners from around the country formed the eleven-member Basketball Association of America at a meeting at the Commodore Hotel in New York. Boston was a charter member.

Q: What team names did the Boston Celtics reject?
A: Walter Brown named his Boston entry "Celtics" after rejecting "Unicorns," "Whirlwinds," and "Olympics." Two New York barnstorming teams (one known as the "Original Celtics") and one Cleveland team had used the name previously.

The first Celtics roster:

Harold Kottman	Virgil Vaughn
Tony Kappen	Al Brightman
Art Spector	Connie Simmons
Warren Fenley	Johnny Simmons
Wyndol Gray	Chuck Connors
Red Wallace	

Q: Who was the Celtics' first opponent?

A: The Celt's first game was played November 2, 1946, at Providence, Rhode Island. The Providence Steamrollers beat them 59–53.

Their home opener was played November 5 at Boston Arena because the rodeo was at Boston Garden. Ticket prices were $1.25 to $2.75, and 4,329 people showed up. The game was delayed after Chuck Connors, later famous as television's *The Rifleman,* shattered one of the ultramodern glass backboards during warmups. When the game finally took place, the Chicago Stags beat the Celts, 57–55.

In their first game at Boston Garden, on November 16, the Celtics beat the Toronto Huskies, 53–49.

The 1946–47 Celtics, coached by John Davis "Honey" Russell, finished last with a 22–38 record.

1947

Led by new acquisitions Ed Sadowski and Dutch Garfinkel, the Celtics finished 20–28, squeaking into the playoffs partially because four teams had folded before the start of the season. They were eliminated by the Chicago Stags in a two-out-of-three series, and Walter Brown fired coach Honey Russell.

Meanwhile, future star Bob Cousy was a freshman on the Holy Cross team, which became the only New England college team to have won the NCAA championship.

1948

Brown hired Alvin "Doggie" Julian, coach of the championship Holy Cross team, to coach the Celtics.

The Celtics finished 25–35, and stockholders urged Brown to fold the team, which had lost $350,000 in its first three years. Brown persuaded them to give him another year.

1949

The BAA merged with six teams from a rival league to form the National Basketball Association, today's NBA.

On December 22, the Celtics beat the Lakers 87–69. Celtic Tony Lavelli not only scored 26 points; he also entertained the crowd at halftime, playing "Lady of Spain" and other classics on his accordion.

The Celtics finished the 1949–50 season with a 22–46 record.

1950

Stockholders sold the team to Walter Brown. The NBA might have folded entirely if not for the Celtics turnaround that began this year.

Q: What was Red Auerbach's first-year salary as coach of the Celtics?
A: Brown hired thirty-two-year-old Arnold "Red" Auerbach to coach the team. Auerbach signed a one-year contract for $10,000.

Auerbach passed up Bob Cousy on draft day, picking 6'11" Charlie Share instead. In the second round the Celtics drafted Chuck Cooper—the first black player ever drafted by an NBA team. After the Celtics drafted Cooper, the Washington Capitals chose Earl Lloyd and the New York Knicks bought the contract of "Sweet-water" Clifton from the Harlem Globetrotters. Lloyd became the first black player actually to appear in an NBA game.

When the Chicago Stags folded, three teams made bids for the team's three top players: Max Zaslofsky, Andy Phillip, and Cousy. The Celtics wanted Zaslofsky, and the players' names were written on slips of paper and drawn from a hat. Auerbach and Brown were dismayed to draw Cousy, who went on to be known as "Mr. Basketball" and to become arguably the best player of all time.

The NBA's first All-Star Game was played at Boston Garden.

The Celtics finished 39–30, but the Knicks beat them in the playoffs.

1951

The Celtics shrewdly acquired Bill Sharman as the player-to-be-named-later in a deal with the Fort Wayne Pistons. Sharman joined the team after spending the last month of the 1951 baseball season with the Brooklyn Dodgers and ultimately became one of the best shooters in NBA history.

The Celtics went 39–27 in the first year of the Cousy-Sharman backcourt, but New York knocked them out of the playoffs.

1954

The Celtics slipped to .500, and Cousy asked to be traded. But Auerbach already had his eye on University of San Francisco center Bill Russell as the solution to the team's shortcomings.

The 24-second clock, invented by Syracuse Nationals owner Danny Biasone, sped up the game, increased the number of shots, and made rebounding more important than ever.

1956

Q: How did the Ice Capades figure in the Celtics' acquisition of Bill Russell?

A: The Rochester Royals had the first draft pick but were reluctant to take Bill Russell because the cost of signing him was likely to be $25,000. Walter Brown agreed to give Royals owner Lester Harrison the Ice Capades for two weeks a year if he would pass up Russell. The Celtics then traded Ed Macauley and Cliff Hagan to St. Louis for the second draft choice. NBA great Oscar Robertson reportedly later observed that St. Louis may have preferred acquiring two white stars rather than Russell.

On April 20 the Celtics drafted Russell. With Cousy and Russell, the Celtics now had two players who remain candidates—along with Michael Jordan, Wilt Chamberlain, and Magic Johnson—to be called the greatest ever. Some aficionados would add Celtics Larry Bird and John Havlicek to the ballot.

Indefatigable Celtic John Havlicek (left) outhustled every other player of his era. Clutch shooter and uncanny passer Larry Bird (right) led the Celtics to NBA championships in 1981, 1984, and 1986.

The Celtics drafted Russell, Tom Heinsohn, and K. C. Jones—three future Hall of Fame members—in one draft.

Russell joined the Celtics in December, after the season had started, because he had first helped the U.S. Olympic basketball team to win a gold medal in Melbourne.

Bill Russell was 6'9" tall. He had outstanding speed and reflexes, outstanding jumping ability, and outstanding basketball intelligence. With Cousy, Sharman, Ramsey, and Heinsohn, Russell gave the Celtics a new kind of basketball team. Red Auerbach and the 1956 Celtics revolutionized defensive play and invented the modern version of fast-breaking, transition basketball.

1957

On April 13, the Celtics beat the St. Louis Hawks, 125–123, in double overtime to win their first NBA championship.

1959

On April 9, the Celtics beat the Minneapolis Lakers, 118–113, for the NBA championship. After a loss in the finals the previous year, when Russell missed two games with an ankle injury, the Celtics began their streak of eight consecutive championships, unequaled by any other professional sports franchise.

1960

Philadelphia Warriors rookie Wilt Chamberlain averaged 37.6 points and 27 rebounds, but Russell and the Celtics beat the Warriors in six games in the playoff semifinals and went on to take the second of their eight consecutive championships.

1961

The Celtics had the greatest team of all time. The Celtics had four Hall of Fame players starting and three more on the bench. Russell, Cousy, Heinsohn, and Sharman started, along with strong and savvy Jim Luscutoff. Hall of Famers on the bench were K. C. Jones, Sam Jones, and Frank Ramsey. Many believe that Tom Sanders, then a rookie, also belongs in the Hall of Fame.

1962

With the final pick in the first round of the draft, the Celtics took John Havlicek, who turned out to be one of the greatest players of all time.

1963

The Celtics beat the Lakers in six games for their fifth consecutive championship. Retiring veteran Cousy and rookie Havlicek each scored 18 in the final game.

During the 1963–64 season, the Celtics became the first NBA team to put five black players on the court at the same time.

1965

The Warriors moved to San Francisco but traded Wilt Chamberlain to the Philadelphia 76ers, so the semifinals of the playoffs featured another battle between Chamberlain and Russell. In the seventh and deciding game, with the Celtics leading 110–109 and 5 seconds left, Havlicek made an outstanding play to steal an inbound pass and preserved the victory for the Celtics. Radio broadcaster Johnny Most kept screaming, "Havlicek stole the ball! Havlicek stole the ball!" helping make this one of the most famous moments in professional sports history.

1967

Russell took over from Auerbach, serving as player-coach. Russell was the first African-American head coach of any major professional sports team in the United States.

The Celtics lost to the 76ers in the playoff semifinals, ending their championship streak at eight. They had won nine championships in ten years. A younger Chamberlain for once got the better of Russell.

1968

Russell's Celtics trailed the 76ers three games to one in the semifinals. But the Celtics won the last three games and went on to beat the Lakers for the Celtics' tenth NBA title.

1969

Chamberlain was traded to the Los Angeles Lakers and again met the now thirty-five-year-old Russell in the finals. The Celtics won in seven games for their eleventh championship.

Russell retired, having won twelve-of-twelve seventh games in a playoff series, four of those against Chamberlain. In all, he had won five of six playoff series against Chamberlain's teams.

1974

The Celtics won championship number twelve in a final against the Milwaukee Bucks with Oscar Robertson and Kareem Abdul-Jabbar.

1976

The Celtics won their thirteenth title. The final against Phoenix included a dramatic triple-overtime win in game five.

1978

The Celtics drafted Larry Bird with the sixth pick in the draft. Bird was eligible because his class was graduating this year, although he had sat out one year and was planning to play another year at Indiana State. If the Celtics had failed to sign Bird by the following year's draft, another team would have been able to draft him. The five teams ahead of the Celtics wouldn't take the risk of drafting Bird and losing him, and ending up with nothing for their high draft choice.

1980

The Celtics traded the first pick overall and the thirteenth pick to Golden State for the third pick overall and (future) Hall-of-Fame center Robert Parish. Golden State took forgettable center Joe Barry Carroll with the top pick—the Celtics took guaranteed Hall-of-Fame forward Kevin McHale with the third choice.

1981

Bird won his first NBA championship, the Celtics' fourteenth.

1982

After the Celtics were beaten by the 76ers in the seventh game of the semifinal series, Boston Garden fans, in a rare display of sportsmanship, chanted "Beat L.A." to Julius "Dr. J" Erving and his teammates in the final minutes.

1983

Q: Who bit whom in the first game of the playoffs?

A: In the first round of the playoffs, in a brawl with Atlanta, seven-footer "Tree" Rollins bit feisty Celtics guard Danny Ainge in the finger. The story is often incorrectly told the other way around.

1984

In one of the roughest NBA finals in history, the Celtics beat the Lakers in seven games for their fifteenth championship. One fight started after Kevin McHale appeared to clothesline Kurt Rambis's neck and chest as he drove for a layup. The series was also noted for Lakers partisans' accusations that the Celtics overheated Boston Garden.

1986

The Celtics acquired Bill Walton and finished with a 40–1 record at Boston Garden. The Celtics won championship number sixteen with relative ease. A highlight of the final series was a fistfight between 7'4" Ralph Sampson and 6'1" Celtics guard Jerry Sichting.

1997

The Celtics finished the season with the worst record in their division, second only to the expansion Vancouver Grizzlies, who were not eligible for the number-one draft pick. The Celtics had acquired a second high pick in an astute trade by coach–general manager M. L. Carr who was replaced at the end of the season in both roles by wunderkind Rick Pitino. Pitino had just coached the Kentucky Wildcats to the NCAA championship, and he had pro experience with the New York Knicks. The Celtics took Chauncey Billups and Ron Mercer in the 1997 NBA draft.

1998

In Pitino's first year as coach and president of the Celtics, the team improved greatly but fell short of making the playoffs. Second-year player Antoine Walker emerged as an all-star and was said to be asking for a multiyear contract for at least $100 million to stay with the team. A long struggle between the NBA Players Association and NBA owners, however, resulted in a lockout, a shortened 1999 season, and a lower cap on superstars' salaries.

BIBLIOGRAPHY

Adams, Russell B., Jr. *The Boston Money Tree.* New York: Thomas Y. Crowell Co., 1977.

Amory, Cleveland. *The Proper Bostonians.* Orleans, Mass.: Parnassus Imprints, 1984.

Beatty, Noelle Blackmer. *Literary Byways of Boston and Cambridge.* Washington, D.C.: Starrhill Press, 1991.

Beebe, Lucius. *Boston and the Boston Legend.* New York: D. Appleton-Century Co., 1935.

"Boston: 12 Moments that Mattered, 1872–1997." *Boston Globe Magazine.* March 2, 1997.

Boston Museum of Fine Arts. *The Bostonians: Painters of an Elegant Age, 1870–1930.* Boston: Museum of Fine Arts, 1986.

Campbell, Robert, and Peter Vanderwarker. *Cityscapes of Boston.* Boston: Houghton Mifflin Co., 1992.

Conway, J. North. *New England Women of Substance: Fifteen Who Made a Difference.* North Attleboro, Mass.: Covered Bridge Press, 1996.

Conway, Lorie. *Boston, The Way It Was.* Boston: WGBH, 1996.

Corbett, William. *Literary New England.* Boston: Faber and Faber, 1993.

Crosby, Irving B. *Boston Through the Ages.* Boston: Marshall Jones Co., 1928.

Cusack, Betty Bugbee. *Collector's Luck: Giant Steps into Prehistory.* Stoneham, Mass.: G. R. Barnstead Printing Co., 1968.

Dalton, Cornelius, John Wirkkala, and Anne Thomas. *Leading the Way: A History of the Massachusetts General Court 1629–1980.* Boston: Office of the Massachusetts Secretary of State, 1984.

Dow, George F., and John H. Edmonds. *The Pirates of the New England Coast, 1630–1730.* New York: Dover Publications, 1996.

Federal Writers' Project of the WPA. *Boston Looks Seaward: The Story of the Port 1630–1940.* Boston: Bruce Humphries, 1941.

Freeland, Richard M. *Academia's Golden Age: Universities in Massachusetts, 1945–1970.* New York: Oxford University Press, 1992.

Goodman, Paul. *The Democratic-Republicans of Massachusetts: Politics in a Young Republic.* Cambridge: Harvard University Press, 1964.

Hall, Max. *The Charles: The People's River.* Boston: David R. Godine, 1986.

Handlin, Oscar. *Boston's Immigrants.* New York: Atheneum, 1968.

Holbrook, Stewart H. *The Old Post Road.* New York: McGraw-Hill Book Co., 1962.

Honig, Donald. *The Boston Red Sox, An Illustrated History.* New York: Prentice-Hall Press, 1990.

Howard, Brett. *Boston, A Social History.* New York: Hawthorn Books, 1976.

Howe, Henry F. *Massachusetts: There She Is—Behold Her.* New York: Harper and Brothers, 1960.

Jennings, John. *Boston, Cradle of Liberty, 1630–1776.* Garden City, N.Y.: Doubleday and Co., 1947.

Jones, Howard Mumford, and Bessie Zaban Jones, eds. *The Many Voices of Boston.* Boston: Little Brown and Co., 1975.

Kates, Emily, and David Kates. *All About the Boston Harbor Islands.* Hingham, Mass.: Hewitts Cove Publish Co., 1993.

Kay, Jane Holtz. *Lost Boston.* Boston: Houghton Mifflin Co., 1980.

Kaye, Clifford A. *The Geology and Early History of the Boston Area of Massachusetts: A Bicentennial Approach.* Washington, D.C.: U.S. Government Printing Office, 1976.

Kelley, Walt. *What They Never Told You About Boston (Or What They Did That Were Lies).* Camden, Maine: Down East Books, 1993.

Kenneally, Christopher. *The Massachusetts Legacy.* Holbrook, Mass.: Adams Publishing, 1995.

Kennedy, Lawrence W. *Planning the City Upon a Hill: Boston Since 1630.* Amherst: University of Massachusetts Press, 1992.

Kenny, Herbert A. *Newspaper Row.* Chester, Conn.: Globe Pequot Press, 1987.

Koren, John. *Boston, 1822–1922: The Story of Its Government and Principal Activities During One Hundred Years.* Boston: City of Boston Printing Department, 1923.

Kruh, David. *Always Something Doing.* Boston: Faber and Faber, 1990.

Lange, James E. T., and Katherine DeWitt Jr. *Chappaquiddick: The Real Story.* New York: St. Martin's Press, 1993.

McCord, David. *About Boston.* Garden City, N.Y.: Doubleday and Co., 1949.

Meyer, William B. "The Worst Weather Disaster in New England History." *Yankee,* January 1997.

Nolen, William A. *The Baby in the Bottle.* New York: Coward, McCann and Geohegan, 1978.

Norton, Elliot. *Broadway Down East: An Informal Account of the Plays, Players and Playhouses of Boston from Puritan Times to the Present.* Boston: Boston Public Library, 1978.

O'Connor, Thomas H. *Bibles, Brahmins and Bosses: A Short History of Boston.* Boston: Trustees of the Public Library of the City of Boston, 1971.

———. *Civil War Boston.* Boston: Northeastern University Press, 1997.

Ramus, Daniel, and Lisa Ramus. *Massachusetts Trivia.* Nashville: Rutledge Hill Press, 1990.

Rosenkrantz, Barbara Guttman. *Public Health and the State: Changing Views in Massachusetts, 1842–1936.* Cambridge: Harvard University Press, 1972.

Russell, Francis. *The Knave of Boston and Other Ambiguous Massachusetts Characters.* Boston: Quinlan Press, 1987.

Russell, Howard S. *Indian New England Before the Mayflower.* Hanover, N.H.: University Press of New England, 1980.

Sammarco, Anthony Mitchell. *Boston: A Century of Progress.* Dover, N.H.: Arcadia Publishing, 1996.

———. *South Boston.* Dover, N.H.: Arcadia Publishing, 1996.

Sandrof, Ivan. *Yesterday's Massachusetts.* Miami: E. A. Seemann Publishing, 1977.

Sarna, Jonathan, and Ellen Smith, eds. *The Jews of Boston.* Boston: Combined Jewish Philanthropies, 1995.

Schofield, William G. *Freedom by the Bay.* Chicago: Rand McNally and Co., 1974.

Seaburg, Carl. *Boston Observed.* Boston: Beacon Press, 1971.

Shaughnessy, Dan. *Evergreen,* New York: St. Martin's Press, 1990.

Simmons, William S. *Spirit of the New England Tribes: Indian History and Folklore, 1620–1984.* Hanover, N.H.: New England University Press, 1986.

Snyder, Louis. *Community of Sound.* Boston: Beacon Press, 1979.

Songini, Marc. *New England's Most Sensational Murders.* North Attleboro, Mass.: Covered Bridge Press, 1995.

Sullivan, Robert F. *Shipwrecks and Nautical Lore of Boston Harbor.* Chester, Conn.: Globe Pequot Press, 1990.

Thomas, David H., et al. *The Native Americans: An Illustrated History.* Atlanta: Turner Publishing Co., 1993.

Tucker, Leonard Louis. *Clio's Consort: Jeremy Belknap and the Founding of the Massachusetts Historical Society.* Boston: Massachusetts Historical Society, 1990.

Vaughan, Alden T. *New England Frontier: Puritans and Indians, 1620–1675.* Third Edition. Norman: University of Oklahoma Press, 1995.

Warner, Sam Bass, Jr. *The Way We Really Live: Social Change in Metropolitan Boston Since 1920.* Boston: Boston Public Library, 1977.

Weston, George F., Jr. *Boston Ways: High, By, and Folk.* Boston: Beacon Press, 1957.

Whitehill, Walter Muir. *Boston, A Topographical History.* Second edition. Cambridge: Harvard University Press, 1968.

———. *Boston in the Age of John Fitzgerald Kennedy.* Norman: University of Oklahoma Press, 1966.

———. *The Museum of Fine Arts, Boston: A Centennial History.* Cambridge: Harvard University Press, 1970.

Wilson, Susan, *Boston Sites and Insights.* Boston: Beacon Press, 1994.

Wright, John W., and Linda Sunshine. *The Best Hospitals in America.* Detroit: Visible Ink Press, 1995.

INDEX

Abbott, Gilbert, 120
Abrams, Marilyn, 164
Adams, Abigail, 23, 40, 41
Adams, Charles Francis, 70
Adams, Charles Francis, Jr., 73
Adams, Henry, 44
Adams, John Quincy, 44
Adams, John Quincy, II, 70
Adams, John, 24, 34, 39, 40, 44, 106, 113
Adams, Russell B., Jr., 64
Adams, Samuel, 24, 26, 33, 89
Adams, Sherman, 180
Affleck, Ben, 165
African Meeting House, 42
Agassiz, Alexander, 72
Agassiz, Elizabeth Cabot Cary, 113
Agassiz, Louis, 113, 137
Agawams, 7
Ainge, Danny, 229
Albert Einstein Educational Foundation, 118
Albright, Tenley, 125
Alcott, Louisa May, 142
Allen, Debbie, 196
Allen, Ethan, 37
American Appliance Company, 79
American Bell, 73
American Civil Liberties Union, 162
American Federation of Labor, 51
American House, 79
American League, x, 208, 209, 220, 221
American Research and Development (ARD),
    80
American Revolution, vii, 36
American Telephone and Telegraph (AT&T),
    73
American Unitarian Association, 44
Ames, Oakes, 71
Ames, Oliver, 71
Ames, Winthrop, 156, 157
Anderson, Harlan, 81
Andrew, John Albion, 91
Andrew, John J., 115
Andros, Edmund, 30, 31
Anthony, Susan B., 33
Antietam, battle of, 49
Aparicio, Luis, 218
Apple Island, 9, 53
Appleton, Frances, 138
Appleton, Nathan, 64, 65
Arbella, 25, 87, 132

Arbuckle, Fatty, 97
Arlington, 20
Arnold Arboretum, 127–29
Arnold, James, 128
Ashbery, John, 148
Ashland, Mass., 202
Astrea, 62
Atlantic Monthly, 134, 136
Attucks, Crispus, 35
Auerbach, Red, x, 224, 225, 228
Augustus, John, 189–90

Back Bay, 7, 16, 68, 70, 107
Bailey, F. Lee, 195
Bakalar, David, 81
Bakalar, Leo, 81
Baker, George Pierce, 156
Baker, Lorenzo, 74
Baldwin, Herb, 177
Bancroft, George, 139
Baptist Society, 153
Barbour, Edmund, 97
Barker Engineering Laboratory, 116, 117
Barnes, Linda, 149
Barnicle, Mike, 182, 183
Barron, Clarence W., 176
Bartlett, John, 137, 141
Bates, Joshua, 106
Baylor, Don, 220
Beacon Hill, 6, 9, 25, 61, 80, 118, 132, *143,*
    147, 161
Beanpot Hockey Tournament, 202
Beardley, Dick, 207
Bell Telephone Company, 72
Bell, Alexander Graham, 58, 72, 171
Benjamin, Asher, 162
Bennett, William, 196
Berenson, Bernard, 126
Bernstein, Leonard, 26, 111
Bigelow, William Sturgis, 123
Billups, Chauncey, 230
Bird Island, 9
Bird, Larry, x, 225, *226,* 229
Blackall, Clarence H., 156
Blackstone, William, 25, 132, 143
Blake, Henry Ingraham, 169
Blakely, Gerald W., 81
Blue Hills, 11
Boda, Michael, 192
Boggs, Wade, 164, 219

Bolt, Beranek, and Newman (BB&N), 58, 83, 84
Bond, Stanley, 195
Booth, Edwin, 155
Booth, John Wilkes, 155
Boott, Kirk, 65
Borden, Lizzie, 172
Boston Advertiser, 172, 173
Boston American, 173
Boston and Lowell Railroad, 66
Boston and Providence Railroad, 66
Boston and Worcester Railroad, 66
Boston Athenaeum, 122
Boston Beaneaters, 208
Boston Beer Company, 84
Boston Bruins, 201
Boston Celtics, x, 164, 201, 202, 222–32
Boston Children's Hospital, 121
Boston College, viii, 19, 117, 119, 197, 202
Boston Common, ix, 15, 16, *18,* 19, 20, 26, 29, 30, 83, 88, 104, *130,* 134, *164*
Boston Courier, 172
Boston Custom House, 135
Boston Duck Tours, 84
Boston Evening Record, 172, 173
Boston Floating Hospital, 18
Boston Fruit Company, 74
Boston Funds, 79
Boston Garden, 223, 224, 230
Boston Globe, 107, *166,* 168, 170, 171, 172, 173, 174, 175, 177, 179, 180, 181, 182, 183
Boston Harbor, vii, 4, 9, 30, 35, 37, 136
Boston Herald, 55, *170,* 171, 172, 173, *176*
Boston Hospital for Women, 121
Boston Journal, 172
Boston Latin School, 26
Boston Light, 11
Boston Lobsters, 201
Boston Lying-In Hospital, 120
Boston Manufacturing Company, 64, 65
Boston Marathon, 202, 202–8
Boston Massacre, 35
"Boston Men," 63
Boston Museum of Fine Arts, 122–26, *125,* 153, 155
Boston Neck, 29
Boston News Letter, 168
Boston Pilgrims, 208
Boston Pops, 109, 110
Boston Port Act, 35
Boston Post, 95, 156, 167, 168, 169, 172, 173, 174, 175, 176, 177, 178, 179, 180
Boston Public Garden, *13*
Boston Public Library, 106–8, 144
Boston Red Sox, x, 85, 121, 147, 164, 201, 202, 208–22

Boston Red Stockings, 208
Boston Redevelopment Authority, 53
Boston Repertory Theater, 152
Boston School Committee, 75, 93
Boston Strangler, ix, 194–95
Boston Symphony Orchestra, 68, 109–11, 154
Boston Tea Party, vii, 35
Boston Theater, 153, 154, 156
Boston Theological Seminary, 118
Boston Transcript, 169, 172, 179
Boston University, viii, 53, 117, 118, 119, 162, 202
Boston University Bridge, 118
Boston University School of Theology, 53
Boston Weekly Messenger, 42
Bosworth, W. Welles, 116
Boylston, Zabdiel, 32
Bradish, Joseph, 187
Bradley, Hugh, 211
Bradstreet, Anne, 132
Brady, George L., 103
Braintree, Mass., 40
Braithwaite, William Stanley, 175
Brandeis, Louis, 74
Brandeis University, viii, 118, 119, 161, 195
Brattle Theater Company, 162
Braves Field, 212
Breed's Hill, 65; battle of, 36
the Brewsters (island), 9
Bridgewater, Mass., 192
Bridgewater State Mental Hospital, 195
Briggs, Arnie, 206
Brigham and Women's Hospital, 196
Brigham Hospital, 121
Brigham, Robert B., 121
Brightman, Al, 222
Brinks robbery (1950), ix, 186, 193–94
British East India Company, 35
Brook Farm, 46, 135, 138
Brooks, John, 43
Brooks, Van Wyck, 148
Brown, John, 49, 141
Brown, Walter, 222, 223, 224
Bryant, Gridley, 66
Buckner, Bill, 220
Bulfinch, Charles, 26, 41, 133, 153, 188
Bull and Finch Pub, 164
Bull, Dixey, 186, 187
Bumpkin Island, 9
Bunch of Grapes Tavern, 35
Bunker Hill, 6; battle of, 36, 37
Bunker Hill Monument, 65
Burfoot, Ambrose, 206
Burlington and Missouri River Railroad, 71
Burns, Anthony, 48, 141, 191
Burroughs, William, 148, 151

Bush, Vannevar, 116
Bussey, Benjamin, 127, 128
Button Island, 9
Buzzard's Bay, 99
Byrd, Richard, 60

Cabot, Cabot, and Forbes, 81
Cabot, Godfrey Lowell, 74, 97, 98
Cabot, Paul Codman, 114
Caffrey, James, 203
Cage, John, 111
Cairnie, Gordon, 145
Calf Island, 9
Calumet and Hecla Copper Mine, 68, 72, 109
Cambridge Bridge, *21*
Cambridge, Mass., 16, 26, 37, 62, *83,* 89,
    112, 116, 132, 136, 137, 139, 141, 142
Cambridge Public Cemetery, 137
Cambridge Street Railway Company, 96
Campbell, John, 168
Cape Cod, 99
Cape Cod Canal, 76
Cape Cod Ship Canal Company, 76
Carbo, Bernie, 219
Carlson, Steve, 20
Carney Hospital, 117
Carney, Andrew, 117
Carney, William, 49
Carr, M. L., 230
Carter, Jimmy, 182
Casey, John M., 156
Castle Island, 9, 136
Castle Square Theater, 156
Cat Island, 9
Central Artery-Tunnel project, 69, 84
Central Park (N.Y.), 16
Chancellorsville, battle of, 38, 50
Channing, William Ellery, 44
Chapman, Raymond A., 160
Chappaquiddick Island, 88, 103
Charles A. Dana Foundation, 121
Charles Playhouse, 162
Charles River, *8,* 17, 118, 120
Charles River Bridge, 14
Charles River dam, 20
Charles River Speedway, 17
Charles Street Jail, 100, *189*
Charles Theater, 152
Charlestown, 14, 17, 25, 43, 45, 65
Chase, Frank, 159
Cheers, 152, 163, 164
Chestnut Hill, 117
Chicago, Burlington, and Quincy Railroad, 71
Child, Lydia Maria, 136
Children's Cancer Research Foundation, 120
Chinatown, 48

Christian Science Church, 50
Christian Science Monitor, 175
Chrysler, Walter P., 75
City Hall Annex, 94
City Hall Plaza, *97*
City Point Aquarium, 94
Civilian Conservation Corps, 96
Claflin, Lee, 117
Clarke, James Freeman, 92
Clemens, Roger, 211, 220, 221
Coakley, Dan, 88, 96
Coakley, Pelletier, and Corcoran, 98
Coconut Grove fire, 19
Coercive Acts, 35
Coffin, Charles A., 73
Cogan, John, 58
Collins, Eddie, 214
Collins, Jimmy, 201, 208
Collins, Patrick, 156
Colonial Theater, 156, 159, 161
Colored American, 173
Columbia, 62
Columbia Trust Company, 76
Columbus, Christopher, 24
Combat Zone, 78, 84
Concord, Mass., 36, 134; battle of, 36
Conigliaro, Tony, 218
Connors, Chuck, 222, 223
Consolidated Hand Lasting Machine
    Company, 74
Coolidge, Calvin, 52, 94
Coolidge, Joseph, 64
Cooper, Chuck, 224
Copland, Aaron, 110
Copley Place Mall, *82*
Copley Plaza Hotel, 97
Copley Square, 107, *108*
Copp's Hill Burying Ground, *41,* 133, 134
Corbett, William, 139
Corcoran, William, 97
Cottage Farm Bridge, 118
Cotton Hill, 8
Cousy, Bob, x, 223, 224, 226, 227
Coytemore, Thomas, 59
Cozzens, James Gould, 148
Credit Mobilier scandal, 71
Croly, Herbert, 145
Cronin, Joe, 214, 215
Cullen, Countee, 148
cummings, e. e., 148
Curley, Arthur, 108
Curley, James Michael, viii, 51, 79, 88, 93,
    94, 97, 98, 99, 100, 101, 102, 103, 108,
    147, 160, 167, 178
Cushing, John Perkins, 64
Cushing, Thomas Perkins, 70

Custom House, 35, 76
Cutler, John, 103

Daily Advertiser, 172
Damon, Matt, 165
Dana, Richard Henry, Jr., 137, 148
Davis, Bette, 119
Davis, Jefferson, 48
Dawes, William, 36
Day, Stephen, 132
de Beaujour, Felix, 60
de Cheverus, Jean Louis anne Magdeleine
    Lefebvre, 42
Declaration of Independence, vii, 31
Dedham, Mass., 66
Deer Island, 9, 10
DeMar, Clarence, 204
Derby, Elias Hasket, 62, 63
Desalvo, Albert, ix, 195
Dever, Paul, 99
Dickinson, Emily, 141, 142
Digital Equipment Corporation, 81
Dinneen, Bill, 209
Dinneen, Joseph, 102
Dix, Dorothea, 46
Dolan, Edmund, 102
Dominion of New England, 30
Donovan, Edward, 92
Dorchester, 6
Dorchester Heights, 37
Downes, William Howe, 145
Doyle, Denny, 219
Drowne, Shem, 33
DuBois, W. E. B., 148
Duffy, Hugh, 208
Dugan, Joe, 213
Dukakis, Michael, 20, 164
Dunn, Edward J., 178
duPont, T. Coleman, 116
Duquette, Don, 221
Dutton, Henry W., 169
Dwyer, Doriot Anthony, 111
Dyer, Mary, *22,* 29

earthquake of 1638, 12; of 1755, 13
Eastman, George, 116
Eddy, Mary Baker, 50, 175
Edelin, Kenneth, 196
Edgell, G. H., 124
Edison, Thomas, 92, 156
Ehmke, Howard, 213
Einstein, Albert, 118
Eliot, Charles, 16
Eliot, Charles W., 116
Eliot, John, 29, 132
Eliot, T. S., 148, 167

Ellsberg, Daniel, 181
Ely, Joseph, 98, 102
E-mail, 84
Emerald Necklace, 16, *18*
Emerson, George Barrell, 127, 128
Emerson, Ralph Waldo, viii, 26, 132, 134,
    136, 137, 138, 140, 148, 154
Erikson, Leif, 24
Esplanade, Charles River, 110
Ether Monument, 104
Evans, Dwight, 219, 220

Faber, Abraham, 193
Fairbanks, Richard, 27
Fair Labor Standards Act, 96
Faithfull, Starr, 94–95
Faneuil, Andrew, 61
Faneuil, Benjamin, 61
Faneuil Hall, 33, 48, 61, 141
Faneuil, Peter, 33, 61, 66
Farber, Sidney, 121, 122
Farmer, Fannie Merritt, 144
Federal League, 212
Federal Street Theater, 153, 161
Fenley, Warren, 222
Fenollosa, Ernest, 122, 123, 140
Fenway Park, x, 168, 176, *210, 211,* 212, 216
Ferncroft Inn, 94
Ferrell, Wes, 214
Fidelity Capital Fund, 82
Fidelity Fund, 81
Fiedler, Arthur, 26, 110, 111
Fields, James T., 136
54th Massachusetts Infantry, 49
Filene, Edward, 75
Filene's Automatic Bargain Basement, 75
Filene's, *57,* 75
financial district, *85*
Fisk, Carlton, 219
Fisk, Jim, 71
Fitzgerald, Ella, 119
Fitzgerald, John F. "Honey Fitz," 75, 76, 88,
    91, 92, 93, 94, 97, 98, 100, 103, 211
Flanagan, Newman, 196
Fleet, Thomas, 133
Fly, William, 187
Flynn, Ray, 84, 164, 196
Forbes, F. Murray, 81
Forbes, John, 67, 68
Forbes, John Murray, 64, 70, 71, 72
Forbes, Malcolm, 73
Forbes, Robert Bennet, 64
Forbes, William, 72, 73
Foreman, Stanley, 55
Forest Hills Cemetery, 147, 162, 192
Fort Devens, 203

Fort Independence, 10, 136
Fort Warren, 10
Fox, John, 179, 180
Foxx, Jimmy, 214, 215
Fradkin, Frederic, 110
Franco, Solomon, 29
Franklin Park, 16
Franklin Park Zoo, 94, 168, 176
Franklin, Benjamin, 26, 61
Frazee, Harry, 213, 214
Freedom Trail, 24
Freeman, Buck, 209
French and Indian War, 33, 34
French, Daniel Chester, 113
Frost, Robert, 148
Fugitive Slave Law of 1850, 48, 141
Fuller, Alvan T., 193
Fuller, Buckminster, 137
Fuller, Margaret, 137

Gage, British Gen. Thomas, 35, 36
Galehouse, Denny, 216
Galen Street Bridge, 14
Gallop's Island, 9, 10
Garciaparra, Nomar, 221
Gardner, Erle Stanley, 148
Gardner, Isabella Stewart, 70, 126
Gardner, John Lowell, 123, 126
Gareau, Jacqueline, 207
Garfinkel, Dutch, 223
Garrett, Oliver B., 95, 178
Garrison, William Lloyd, 33, 44, 45, 136,
   167, 169
Garrity, W. Arthur, 54
Gaugengigl, Ignaz Marcel, 142
Gazette, 168
Geary, Susan, 173
General Electric, 73
General Motors Corporation, 75, 93
George's Island, 9, 10
Gericke, Wilhelm, 109
Gerry, Elbridge, 42
Gibb, Roberta, 205
Gilday, William, 195
Gillam, James, 187
Gillette, King C., 75
Gillette Razor Company, 75
Godkin, E. L., 39
Goldberg, Lawrence R., 95, 178
Goldfine, Bernard, 180
Goldstein, Israel, 118
Gompers, Samuel, 52
Good, Sarah, 31, 135
Gordon, Joe, 215
Gordon, Ruth, 161
Gorman, Miki, 206

Gosnold, Bartholomew, 25
Gould, Jay, 72, 73
Government Center, *97*
Governor's Island, 9, 10, 53
Granite Railway Company, 66
Grape Island, 9
the Graves (island), 9
Gray, Asa, 128, 169
Gray, Wyndol, 222
Great Bridge (Harvard Square), 14
Great Colonial Hurricane of 1635, 12
the Great Fire of 1872, 71
Great Hurricane of 1938, 19
Great Molasses Flood of 1919, 4, 18
Great Western Railroad, 68
Green, Elijah "Pumpsie," 217
Green, Howard, 116
Green Island, 9, 10
Griffin's Wharf, 35
Griffith, D. W., 155, 158
Grimke, Angelina, 136
Grimke, Sarah, 136
Grolier Bookshop, 145
Grove, Lefty, 214
Grozier, Edward A., 172
Grozier, Edwin, 174, 175, 176
Grundmann, Otto, 123
Gustafson, Carl Einar, 122

Hagan, Ed, 225
Hale, Edward Everett, *130*
Haley, Alex, 147
Half Moon Island, 9
Hall, Bob, 206
Hancock, John, 26, 35, 37, 40, 61, 62, 90,
   153
Hancock, Thomas, 61, 62
Hangman's Island, 9
Harris, Benjamin, 168
Hart, Moss, 156
Harte, Bret, 142
Harvard Bridge, 16
Harvard Business School, 114
Harvard Divinity School, 50, 113
Harvard, John, 27, 112, 113
Harvard Lampoon, 52
Harvard Law School, 113
Harvard Medical School, 113, 121
Harvard Square, 14, 89, 132, 145
Harvard Stadium, 114
Harvard University, viii, 26, 27, 33, 76, 90,
   112–14, 122, 131, 132, 135, 137, 138,
   144, 146, 148, 149, 156, 157, 162, 185,
   190, 191, 193, 199, 202
Harvard University–Museum of Fine Arts
   Egyptian Expedition, 123

Harvard Yard, 113
Hassam, Frederick Childe, 143
Hathorne, John, 135
Havlicek, John, x, 225, *226*, 227
Hawkins, Thomas, 187
Hawley, Beatrice, 138
Hawthorne, Nathaniel, viii, 135, 136, 147
Hay, Robert, 123
Hayden, Harriet, 67
Hayden, Lewis, 67
Hayden, Stone, and Company, 76
Hayes, Roland, 110
Head of the Charles Regatta, 202
Hearst, William Randolph, 173
Heart, Frank, 83
Heat Wave of 1911, 17
Heinsohn, Tom, 226, 227
Helprin, Mark, 148
Hemenway, Augustus, 71
Hendricks, Thomas, 95
Hennessy, Patricia, 198
Henry, Patrick, 34
Henschel, George, 109
Herne, James A., 155
Herschel, Clemens, 128
Herter, Christian, 98
Hibbard, George, 93
Hibbens, Ann, 29
Hicks, Louise Day, 180
Higginson, Francis, 3
Higginson, George, 67, 68, 109
Higginson, Henry Lee, 68, 73, 109, 109–10, 156
Higginson, Stephen, 62
Higginson, Thomas Wentworth, 141, 142
High School of Commerce, 94
HMS *Guerriere,* 43
Hoar, Sherman, 113
Hog Island, 9
Holbrook, Donald, 79–80
Holmes, Oliver Wendell, 15, 43, 49, 134, 135, 136, 148, 154
Holmes, Oliver Wendell, Jr., 49, 135, 148
Homer, Winslow, 137
Hooker, Joseph, 38, 50
Hopkins, Pauline, 173
Houghton Mifflin, 136
Houson, Edwin J., 73
Howe, British Gen. William, 37
Howe, Julia Ward, 135, 137, 141, 147
Howe, Samuel Gridley, 45
Howells, William Dean, 137, 142
Hoyt, Charles H., 156
Hoyt, Waite, 213
Hubbard, Gardiner Greene, 72
Hubbard, William, 12

Huff, George, 210
Hull, Edward, 187
Hull, John, 29, 60
Humphrey, Hubert, 181
Hunt, William Morris, 123
Huntington Avenue Grounds, 208
Hurley, Joseph "Chowderhead," 98
Hussein, Ibrahim, 207
Hutchinson, Anne, 26, 27, 87
Hutchinson, Thomas, 34
Hyde, Elaine, 199

Industrial Electronics Laboratory, 80
International Match Corporation, 77
Internet, viii, 58, 83
Irish immigration, viii, 46–47
Isabella Stewart Gardner Museum, ix, 118, 126–27; robbery, 197–98
IWW, 51

Jackson, James, 119
Jackson, Patrick Tracy, 64, 65, 66, 70
Jacobs, Harriet A., 137, 140
Jamaica Plain, 147, 162, 192
Jamaica Pond, 16
James, Alice, 137
James, Henry, 137, 139, 142
James, William, 137, 148
Jefferson, Thomas, 44
Jennings, John, 7
Jewett, Henry, 158, 159
Jewett, John P., 140
Jimmy Fund, 120, 121, 122
John Hancock Financial Services Corporation, 207
John Hancock Mutual Life Insurance Company, 80
Johnson, Byron Bancroft "Ban," 208
Johnson, Edward C., II, 81, 82
Johnson, Edward C., III, "Ned," 82
Johnson, Philip, 108
Jolson, Al, 160
Jones, K. C., 226, 227
Jones, Margaret, 28
Jones, Same, 227
Jordan Marsh Company, 67, 171
Jordan, Bruce, 164
Jordan, Eben, 170, 173
Julian, Alvin "Doggie," 223

Kahal Kadosh Ohabei Shalom, 46
Kakuzo, Okakura, 123
Kappen, Tony, 222
Katzmann, Fred, 192
Kaufman, George S., 156
Kean, Edmund, 153

Keayne, Robert, 58
Keith, B. F., 156
Kelly, John "the Elder," 205
Kelly, John "the Younger," 205
Kennedy, Edward M. "Ted," 76, 88, 103
Kennedy, John F., 24, 33, 54, 75, 76, 88, 91, 94, 126, 179
Kennedy, Joseph P., 76, 179
Kennedy, Joseph P., Jr., 76
Kennedy, Robert, 76
Kennedy, Rose Fitzgerald, 76
Kidd, William, 187
Kilty, Jerome, 162
Kimihara, Kenji, 205
King Philip, 30; King Philip's War, 10, 30
King's Chapel, 14, 28
King, Martin Luther, Jr., 53
Knowles, Joe, 175
Knox, Henry, 37
Koch, Jim, 84
Kopechne, Mary Jo, 88, 103
Kottman, Harold, 222
Kreuger, Ivar, 77
Kuscsik, Nina, 206
Kyriakides, Stylianos, 204

LaFlesche, Suzette, 33
Lalas, Alexi, 201
Land, Edwin H., 80
Lang, V. R., 137
Langlee's Island, 9
Langton, Jane, 149
The Last Hurrah, viii, 88, 99, 147, 157
Lavelli, Tony, 224
law banning all forms of contraception, 54
Lawrence, Amos, 66
Lawrence, Amos Adams, 68
Lee, Higginson, and Company, 67, 68, 73, 74–75, 77, 109
Lee, John C., 67
Legal Securities Corporation, 102
Leno, Jay, 165
Leonard, Dutch, 212, 213
Levine, Faye, 138
Lewis, Duffy, 213
Lexington, Mass., vii; battle of, 36
Lexington Green, 36
Liberator, 44, 45, 136, 167, 169
Liberty, 35
Lido Venice, 162
Lighthouse Island, 9, 11
Lindbergh, Charles, 19
Little Calf Island, 9
Little Hog Island, 9
the "little ice age," 13
Lockhart, Keith, 111

Loeb Drama Center, 162
Logan Airport, 10, 20, 21, 52, 81
Logan, Edward L., 81
Lomasney, Martin, 92, 93, 94, 95, 96, 101
Lonborg, Jim, 218
Longfellow House, 137
Longfellow, Henry Wadsworth, 15, 134, 137, 141
Lorz, Fred, 203
Lovell's Island, 9, 11
Low, Ned, 187, 188
Lowell, Abbot Lawrence, 193
Lowell, Amy, 137, 145, 146, 157
Lowell, Charles Russell, 70
Lowell, Francis Cabot, 57, 63, 65, 169
Lowell, Guy, 124
Lowell Institute, 115, 123, 169
Lowell, James Russell, 134, 136, 137, 146
Lowell, John, 62, 63, 64, 123, 169
Lowell, John Amory, 66, 113
Lowell, Pervical, 123
Lowell, Robert, 133, 138, 146
Luscutoff, Jim, 227
Lyman, Theodore, Jr., 45
Lynn, Fred, 219

McCarthy, Joe, 216
Macauley, Ed, 225
McCormack, Mary Ellen, 52
McDermott, John J., 202
MacDonald, Arch, 179
McDonald, Ronald, 203
McDonough, William, 189
McElroy, John, 117
McGovern, George, 24, 54
McGraw, John, 209
McGuire, Deacon, 210
McHale, Kevin, 164, 229, 230
McKim, Charles, 107, 144
McKim, Mead, and White, 107, 109, 114
McLean Psychiatric Hospital, 138
McMasters, William, 176
McMonnie's Frederick William, 144
McNamara, John, 221
McNary, Bill, 100
the "Magazine Club," 134
Maicaway, 102
Mailer, Norman, 148
Malcolm X, 147
Mann, Horace, 45, 46
Mansfield, Frederick W., 160
Maquire, "Pea Jacket," 99, 100
Marquand, John P., 145
Marsh, Daniel L., 118
Marsh, Eben, 67
Marshall, John, 123

Mason and Hamlin Organ Company, 171
Mason, John, 27
Massachusetts Bank, 62
Massachusetts Bay Colony, 30
Massachusetts Bay Company, 25
Massachusetts Court of Assistants, 186
Massachusetts Electric Company, 76
Massachusetts General Court, 25, 26, 27, 29, 47, 89, 90, 112
Massachusetts General Hospital, 65, 104, 119, 120, 121
Massachusetts Hospital Life Insurance Company, 65
Massachusetts Institute of Technology (MIT), viii, 16, 52, 80, 81, 85, 114–17, *115*, 122
Massachusetts Investors Trust, 79
Massachusetts Medical College, 190
Massachusetts Mercury, 169
Massachusetts Parking Authority, 103
Massachusetts Society for the Suppression of Intemperance, 43
Massachusetts State House, 50
Massachusetts Supreme Court, 47, 89–90
Massachusetts Temperance Society, 43
Massachusetts tribe, 7
Massasoit, 30
Mather, Cotton, 12, 26, 29, 32, 132, 133, 134, 148
Mather, Increase, 132, 133, 148
Matzeliger, Jan, 74
Mays, Carl, 213
Mederos, Richard W., 199
Melville, Herman, 25
Mercer, Ron, 230
Merchant, Freddy, 203
Merrimack Manufacturing Company, 65
Merwin, W. S., 147
Messiaen, Olivier, 111
Metacom, 30
Metcalfe's Mill, 202
Metropolitan District Commission, 16
Metropolitan Park Commission, 16
Middlesex University, 118
Millen, Irving, 193
Millen, Murton, 193
Miller, Tom, 206
Millet, Jean François, 123
Minot's light, 15
Mission Hill, 196
"A Modell of Christian Charity," 87
Mohawk Packing Company, 102
Money, 64
Monis, Judah, 33
Montrose, 17
Moody, Paul, 64
Moon Island, 9

Moore, Eugenia, 199
Morgan, J. P., 73
Morgan, Joe, 221
Morison, Samuel Eliot, 144, *146*
Morse, Edward Sylvester, 122
Morton, William, 120
Most, Johnny, 228
Mother Goose, 133
Motley, John Lothrop, 139
Mott, Lucretia, 136
Mount Auburn Cemetery, 136, 140
Mount Benedict School for Girls, 45
Mount Vernon, 8
Mount Vernon Place Congregational Church, 118
Mount Whoredom, 9
Muck, Karl, 110
Munsey, Frank, 173
Murphy, George R. 101
Mystic Wharf, 17

Nabokov, Vladimir, 146
Narragansett Bay, 27
Narragansetts, 7, 30
Nash, Charles W., 75
Nassar, George, 195
Natick, 29, 132
National Association for the Advancement of Colored People (NAACP), 54
National Bell Telephone Company, 72
National Guard, 51
Ndeti, Cosmas, 207
New England Asylum for the Blind, 45
New England Blizzard (WBL), 201
New England Emigrant Aid Company, 68
New England Journal of Medicine, 119
New England Patriots, 201
New England Prospects, 11
New England Repertory Theater, 161
New England Telephone Company, 72
New England Watch and Ward Society, 97
New York Times Company, 182
Newkirk, Cyrus, 173
Newkirk, Newton, 173
Newman, Robert, 32
Newton, 6
Newtowne, Mass., 26, 112
Nichols, Malcolm E., 160
Nipmucs, 30
Nix's Mate, 9
Nixon, Richard M., 24, 54, 168, 182
Nobel Prize, 147
Noddle's Island, 9
Norfolk Prison Colony, 147
Norman's Woe, 15
Norris, Jim, 205

North Church, 14
North End, 133, 134
North End Park, 18
Northeastern University, 118, 202
Norton, Charles Eliot, 122
Norton, Elliot, 161
Nut Island, 9

O'Brien, Conan, 165
O'Casey, Sean, 160
O'Connor, Edwin, 147
O'Connor, Julia, 52
Ogle, Charles, 157
O'Keefe, "Specs," 194
Oksanen, Eino, 205
Old Corner Book Store, 118, 134
Oldham, John, 27
Old Howard Athenaeum, 154
the Old Howard, 154, 155, 160, 162
Old North Church, 32
"Old Ironsides," 43, 135
Old State House, 31, 33, 34, 45, 89, 90, 118
Olmsted, Frederick Law, 16, 129
Olsen, Kenneth, 81
Olson, Charles, 148
O'Meara, Stephen, 173
O'Neill, Albert "Dapper," 196
O'Neill, Eugene, 147, 160, 162
O'Neill, Thomas "Tip," 99, 164
Orpheum Theater, 154
Osborne, Sarah, 31, 135
Otis, Harrison Gray, 45
Otis, James, 34
Otter, 62
Ottway, Thomas, 152
Outer Brewster, 11

Parish, Robert, 229
Park Street Station, 53
Parker, Harvey, 48
Parker House, 99, 134, 147
Parker, Robert, 148
Parker, Theodore, 48, 106, 141
Parkham, Francis, 137, 139, 148, 190
Parkman, George, 190
Parris, Alexander, 66
Parris, Elizabeth, 31
Parris, Samuel, 31
Patriarca, Raymond, 98
Pawtuckets, 7
Payne, William, 31
Peabody, Elizabeth Palmer, 137
Pearce, Howard, 203
Peddock's Island, 9
Pelletier, Joseph, 97
Pemberton Hill, 66

Pemberton Peak, 8
Pemberton Square, 66
Pennacooke, 7
Pennock, Herb, 213
Pentagon Papers, 168, 181
People Before Highways march, 83
Pequot War of 1637, 27
Perkins, Charles E., 71
Perkins, Francis, 96
Perkins School for the Blind, 45, 62, 68
Perkins, Thomas Handasyd, 45, 62, 66, 68, 113
Peter Bent Brigham Hospital, 120, 121
Peters, Andrew James, 94, 95
Petersham, Mass., 40
Petter, Edwin Burr, 161
Phillip, Andy, 224
Phillippe, Deacon, 209
Phillips, John, 43
Phillips, Wendell, 26, 141
Phils, William, 31
Pitino, Rich, x, 230
Plant, Mathias, 13
Plath, Sylvia, 138, 145
Pocasset, 30
Poe, Edgar Allan, 10, 135, 169
Pokanokets, 7
Polaroid Corporation, 80, 82
Polk, James K., 47
Pollard, Benjamin, 43
Ponzi, Charles, 77, 176; Ponzi scheme, 77
Pormort, Philemon, 26
Portland Gale, 17
Portner, Paul, 164
Pound, Ezra, 140, 145
Power, Katherine Ann, 195
Praying Towns, 29, 30
Prendergast, Maurice, 145
Presbyterians, 28
Prescott, Samuel, 36
Prescott, British Col. William, 36
Prescott, William Hickling, 138
Preston, Andrew, 74
Preston, William G., 115, 128
Prohibition, 10, 79, 178
Proposition 2½, 55
Prose, Francine, 148
Provident Institution for Savings in the Town of Boston, 64
Prudential Center, 82
Prudential Insurance Company, 82
Public Gardens Foot Bridge, 128
Publick Occurrences: Both Foreign and Domestic, 168
Pulitzer Prize, 111, 144, 145, 146, 176, 180, 182

Purity Distilling Company, 18
Pusey, Nathan, 114

Quelch, John, 187
Quincy Market, 66
Quincy, Josiah, 43, 90, 91
Quinn, Bob, 214

Raccoon Island, 9
Ragged Island, 9
Rainsford Island, 9, 11
Ramsey, Frank, 226, 227
Rand, Sally, 116
Randolph, Edward, 30
Rathbone, Perry, 125
Raytheon Manufacturing Company, 79, 84,
   116
Reisner, George A., 123
Repertory Theater of Boston, 159, 161
Report of the Sanitary Commission, 47
Republic, 92
Revere, Paul, 24, 32, 36, 40, 41, 42, 202
Rhode Island, 27, 29
Rice, Jim, 220
Rich, Adrienne, 148
Rich, Isaac, 117
Richardson, H. H., 16
Ripley, George, 46, 138
Ripley, Sophia, 46, 138
Riverbank Development Company, 70
Roberts, Benjamin F., 47
Roberts, Eugene, 206
Roberts, Pasha, 85
Roberts, Sarah, 47
Robinson, Edward Arlington, 148
Robinson, Harriet, 65
Rodgers, Bill, *200,* 206
Rogers, Henry Darwin, 115
Rogers, Malcolm, 126
Rogers, William Barton, 114–15
Roosevelt, Franklin D., 19, 96, 101
Roosevelt, Theodore, 119
Ross, Denman W., 124
Rowe, John, 52
Roxbury, 6, 147
Ruiz, Rosie, 207
Russell, Bill, x, 225, 226, 227, 228
Russell, Francis, 100
Russell, John Davis "Honey," 223
Russell, Thomas, 62
Ruth, George Herman "Babe," x, 212, 213
Ryan, "Toodles," 94
Ryan, Kate, 153

Sacco, Nicola, 192–93
Sachar, Abram, 119

the Sacred Cod, 54
Sadowski, Ed, 223
Sailor Island, 9
Salazar, Alberto, 207
Saltonstall, Leverett, 98
Samuel Adams beer, 58, 84
Sanders, Thomas, 72
Sanders, Tom, 227
Sanderson, Richard, 29
Santayana, George, 26, 148
Sargent, Charles Sprague, 128, 129
Sargent, John Singer, 144
the "Saturday Club," 134
Saturday Evening Gazette, 172
Saturday Evening Post, 154
Saugus, Mass., 116
Savage, Emma, 114–15
Saxe, Susan, 195
Schama, Simon, 191
Schiraldi, Calvin, 220
Schon, Nancy, *149*
School of the Museum of Fine Arts, 123
Schooler, William, 187
Schroeder, Walter, 195
Science and Health, 50
Scollay Square, 51, 54, 163
Semple, Jock, 206
Sentry Hill, 9
Sert, Jose Luis, 119
Sewall, Samuel, 60, 133
Sexton, Anne, 148
Sharman, Bill, 225, 226, 227
Shattuck, Lemuel, 47
Shaw, George Bernard, 119
Shaw, Quincy Adams, 72
Shaw, Robert Gould, 49, 190
Shawmut Peninsula, 6, 8, 25
Shays, Daniel, 40
Sheep Island, 9
Sheigematsu, Morio, 205
Sheldon, Asa G., 66
Shore, Ernie, 213
Shubert Theater, 157, 163
Shurtleff, Arthur, 50
Sichting, Jerry, 230
Simmons College, 118
Simmons, Connie, 222
Simmons, John, 118
Simmons, Johnny, 222
Simon, Neil, 156
Sims, Thomas, 191
Sinnot, Richard, 132
Sinnott, Richard J., 163
Slate Island, 9
slave ship, 44, 152
slave trade, 61

slavery, 23, 33, 39, 47, 48, 70, 133, 136, 140, 167, 191
slaves, 31, 32, 48, 60, 61, 133, 135, 188, 190
Sleeper, Jacob, 118
Smibert, John, 33
Smith, Al, 101
Smith, John, 7, 25
Smith, Norman, 21
Smith, Patricia, 182, 183
Smith, Sara, 149
Snake Island, 9
the "Snow Hurricane" of 1804, 14
Social Security Act, 96
Society for Collegiate Instruction of Women, 113
Solano, Louisa, 145
Sons of Liberty, vii, 34, 35, 89
South Boston, 165
South Braintree, 192
Spaulding, John T., 124
Speaker, Tris, 212
Spectacle Island, 9
Spector, Art, 222
Spy Pond, 20
St. Botolph Club, 144
Stackpole, J. J., 67
Stahl, Chick, 210
Stahl, Jake, 211
Stamp Act, 34
Stanley, Bob, 220
State House, 86
Stein, Gertrude, 148
Stephens, Gene, 217
Stevens, Wallace, 148
Stewart, Michael, 192
Stockwell, Stephen N., 170
Stone, Lucy, 136
Storrow, James Jackson, 93
Storrow, James Jackson, Jr., 74, 75
Stowe, Harriet Beecher, 140
Strong, Caleb, 90
Stuart, Carol DiMaiti, 196
Stuart, Charles "Chuck," 196–97
Stuart, Gilbert, 133
Stubbins, Hugh, 162
Students for a Democratic Society, 114
Sturgis, Russell, 64
Suffolk Law School, 197
Suh, Yun Bok, 204
Sullivan, James, 90
Sullivan, William, 158
Sumner, Charles, 47
Switzer, Kathy, 205

Tanzi, Rudolph, 121, 122
Tapply, William G., 149

Task Force on Battered Women and Self-Defense, 198
Taylor, Charles H., 170, 173, 177
Taylor, James, 138
Taylor, W. Davis, 179
Taylor, William O., 177, 179
Taylor, Zachary, 170
Ted Williams Tunnel, 85
Tew, Thomas, 187
Tewksbury, William, 10
Thayer, Webster, 192, 193
Theater Comique, 157
Theodore Dreiser, 152
Thomas, Alice, 59
Thompson, John F., 103
Thompson, John L., 88
Thompson's Island, 9
Thomson, Elihu, 73
Thomson-Houston Electric Company, 73
Thoreau, Henry David, 136, 140, 141, 148
Tiant, Luis, 164
Ticknor and Fields, 136
Ticknor, William, 136
Tillich, Paul, 53
Tisdale, Elkanah, 42
Tituba, 31, 135
Tobin Bridge, 197
Tobin, Maurice J., 178
Tomaszweski, Stanley, 19
Tomita, Kojiro, 123
Tomlinson, Ray, 84
Torres-Carbonnel, Jose, 199
Townshend Acts, 35
Toy Theater, 157, 158
Tracerlab, Inc., 80
the Transcendental Club, 137
Transitron Electronics Corporation, 81
Treaty of Paris, 34
Tremont Street, 28
Tremont Street Subway, 51
Tremont Temple, 49
Tremont Theater, 153, 155
the triangular trade, 60
Trickey, Henry G., 172
Trimountain, 8, 66
Tsai, Gerald, Jr., 81, 82
Tufts, Charles, 117
Tufts College (University), viii, 117
Tufts Dental School, 117
Tufts Medical School, 117
Tukey, Francis, 191
Twain, Mark, 106

Underground Railroad, 67
Underhill, John, 27
Unglaub, Bob, 210

Union Oyster House, 44
Union Pacific Railroad, 73
Unitarian Christianity, 44
United Fruit Company, 74
United Shoe Machinery Corporation, 74
University of Kansas, 68
Updike, John, ix, 146, 148
Urich, Robert, 148
Ursuline Convent, 45
USS *Constitution*, 24, 41, 43, 135, *139*

Valeri, Richard, 195
Vanderbilt, William, 72
Vanzetti, Bartolomeo, 192–93
Vaughn, Mo, 221, 222
Vaughn, Virgil, 222
Vergoose, Elizabeth, 133
Very, Jones, 138
Veterans' Theater Workshop, 162
Vietnam War, 54

Wakarusa, Kan., 68
Walker, Antoine, 230
Walker, George, 111
Wallace, Red, 222
Walpole State Prison, 194
Walter, Cornelia Wells, 169
Walter, Lynde Minshul, 169
Waltham, Mass., 64, 70, 118–19
Walton, Bill, 230
Wampanoags, 7
Wang Center, *150*
War of 1812, 43, 139
Warren, Edward Perry, 123
Warren, John C., 119
Warren, John Collins, 43
Washington, George, 37, 133, 137
Washington, Martha, 133, 137
Watch and Ward Society, 144, 155, 160
Watertown, 62
Watertown Square, 14
Watson, Thomas, 72
WBZ, 177, 179, *180, 181*
Webb, Mel, 216
Webline Communications Corporation, 85
Webster, Daniel, 170
Webster, John White, 190–91
WEEI, 98
Weiman, Henry Nelson, 53
Weld, Charles Goddard, 123
Weld, Eleazar, 127
Weld, Joseph, 127
Weld, William, 198

Wellesley College, 146
Wells, H. G., 119
Wentworth, James, 169
West Boston Bridge, 14
West Roxbury, 6, 49, 135, 138
Western Union, 72
Wetherley, Tee, 187
WGBH, 169
Whalen, "One-armed Peter," 99
Wheatley, Phillis, 133
White, Kevin, 180
Whittier, John Greenleaf, 134, 141
Wilbur Theater, 158, 161
Wilder, Thornton, 161
Willard, Solomon, 66
Williams, Abigail, 31
Williams, Accelynne, 199
Williams, John, 111, 187
Williams, Robin, 165
Williams, Roger, 26
Williams, Ted, x, 85, 147, 214, 215, 216, 217
Williams, Tennessee, 161, 163
Wilson, Andrew, 84
Winship, Laurence L., 175, 179
Winship, Thomas, 180
Winsor, Justin, 107
Winthrop, John, 14, 25, 27, 28, 59, 87, 89, 127, 186
Wister, Owen, 148
WNAC, 102
Wolfe, Thomas, 148
Wood, Smoky Joe, 212
Wood, William, 11
Woollcott, Alexander, 158
Works Progress Administration, 161
World Series, x, 209, 212, 213, 214, 216, 218, 220
World War I, 51, 79, 81, 110, 203, 213
World War II, 10, 42, 52, *86*
Wright, Steven, 165
Wrigley Field, x

Xerox, 82

Yastrzemski, Carl, x, 218, 220
Yawkey, Thomas Austin, 214
Yeats, William Butler, 157
"the Year without a Summer," 15
Young, Cy, 208, 209, 210

Zaslofsky, Max, 224
Zenga, Walter, 201